Roman Special Forces
and Special Ops

By the same author:

Sea Eagles of Empire

Empire State: How the Roman Military Built an Empire

Septimius Severus in Scotland

Roman Legionaries

Ragstone to Riches

Julius Caesar: Rome's Greatest Warlord

Old Testament Warriors

Pertinax: The Son of a Slave Who Became Roman Emperor

Romans at War

Roman Britain's Missing Legion: What Really Happened to IX Hispana?

Roman Conquests: Britain

Ancient Greeks at War

Alexander the Great vs Julius Caesar: Who Was the Greatest Commander in the Ancient World?

Roman Britain's Pirate King

Roman Special Forces and Special Ops

Speculatores, Exploratores, Protectores and Areani in the Service of Rome

Simon Elliott

Pen & Sword
MILITARY

First published in Great Britain in 2023 by
Pen & Sword Military
An imprint of
Pen & Sword Books Ltd
Yorkshire – Philadelphia

Copyright © Simon Elliott 2023

ISBN 978 1 39909 092 6

The right of Simon Elliott to be identified as Author of this work has been asserted by him in accordance with the Copyright, Designs and Patents Act 1988.

A CIP catalogue record for this book is
available from the British Library.

All rights reserved. No part of this book may be reproduced or transmitted in any form or by any means, electronic or mechanical including photocopying, recording or by any information storage and retrieval system, without permission from the Publisher in writing.

Typeset by Mac Style
Printed in the UK by CPI Group (UK) Ltd, Croydon, CR0 4YY.

Pen & Sword Books Limited incorporates the imprints of Atlas, Archaeology, Aviation, Discovery, Family History, Fiction, History, Maritime, Military, Military Classics, Politics, Select, Transport, True Crime, Air World, Frontline Publishing, Leo Cooper, Remember When, Seaforth Publishing, The Praetorian Press, Wharncliffe Local History, Wharncliffe Transport, Wharncliffe True Crime, White Owl and After the Battle.

For a complete list of Pen & Sword titles please contact

PEN & SWORD BOOKS LIMITED
47 Church Street, Barnsley, South Yorkshire, S70 2AS, England
E-mail: enquiries@pen-and-sword.co.uk
Website: www.pen-and-sword.co.uk

Or

PEN AND SWORD BOOKS
1950 Lawrence Rd, Havertown, PA 19083, USA
E-mail: Uspen-and-sword@casematepublishers.com
Website: www.penandswordbooks.com

Dedicated to my son Alexander, my history, gaming and modelling partner in crime!

Contents

Introduction		viii
Chapter 1	What Are Special Operations and Special Forces?	1
Chapter 2	Specialist and Elite Roman Troops	17
Chapter 3	Intelligence Gathering in the Roman World	36
Chapter 4	*Speculatores* and *Exploratores*	57
Chapter 5	*Protectores*	78
Chapter 6	*Areani* and Later Roman Special Forces	95
Conclusion		121
Appendix: Enemies of the Roman Republic and Empire		124
References and Bibliography		145
Index		155

Introduction

The term 'special forces' is one of the most widely known, yet least understood, when describing certain types of specialized military combat unit today. Names like Special Air Service (SAS), US Navy Sea Air Land (SEAL) or Spetsnaz immediately spark attention and interest. However, such troop types are not a modern phenomenon, with warriors operating outside the context of mainstream military endeavour long being a feature of warfare, including in the ancient world.

Special forces, both now and then, are associated with a wide variety of clandestine roles, frequently deep behind enemy lines and often in the opposing homeland itself. Their activities have traditionally included intelligence gathering and stealthy reconnaissance, the disruption of chains of command and lines of supply, and the targeted assassination of opposing decision takers. To perform such specialist tasks, special forces are also associated with certain specific traits, for example elite selection and training, very high levels of motivation, and the ability to survive in the most extreme environments and situations. More often than not, their activities have also been deniable by their political and military masters.

In the ancient world, the Romans are by far the most visible in their use of special forces, and of the widest possible kinds too. Any reader of Roman military history or historical fiction will be familiar with a whole raft of enigmatic names used to detail such 'special' units. Think of the *frumentarii*, *speculatores*, *exploratores*, *protectores* and *areani*, all covered in this book. Here I tell their story in detail for the very first time, allowing these elite warriors to emerge from the mists of history and take their true place in the wider story of the Roman military.

To achieve this, the book begins with this Introduction where I detail the wide variety of sources used, and provide some key definitions to allow the reader to fully understand what follows. Chapter 1 then moves on to explain what special operations and special forces actually are, detailing them in a modern context to help benchmark later descriptions of their

Roman progenitors. At the end of this chapter I then set out a series of criteria to determine if a given military unit in the Roman world was the equivalent of what today we would call special forces. This will then be used at the close of all subsequent chapters to allow a determination to be made about whether the unit types covered there were 'special' or not.

In Chapter 2 I consider specific specialist and elite troops in mainstream Roman military service. This allows a discussion about whether they, in any sense, can be considered 'special', and also provides a benchmark for the specific special force candidates that follow. Chapter 3 then begins our focus on such units, starting with Roman intelligence services (for example the *frumentarii*, *agentes in rebus* and *notarii*), with Chapter 4 then covering the *speculatores* and *exploratores*, Chapter 5 the *protectores* and Chapter 6 the *areani* and later Roman special operations. The conclusion then considers the findings as a whole, enabling a final determination of which troop types in Roman service were truly special forces in the modern sense.

The book closes with an appendix providing more detail of the various key opponents faced by the Republic and empire where Roman special forces may have played a role.

Moving on to sources, I have used the widest possible selection ranging from ancient to very recent. In terms of the former, some common texts have proved most useful given their often-detailed descriptions of classical and early medieval warfare. These include Cornelius Tacitus with his *Annals*, *Histories* and *Agricola*, Gaius Suetonius with his *Twelve Caesars*, and Appian with his *Roman History*. As always, Cassius Dio with his own *Roman History*, Herodian with his *History of the Roman Empire*, and the now anonymous *Historia Augusta* are also key primary sources. The latter is a collection of biographies of Roman Emperors, junior colleagues, designated heirs and usurpers from the accession of Hadrian in AD 117 through to the accession of Diocletian in AD 284. Written towards the end of the fourth century AD in Latin, modern scholars believe it was based on a single work dating to the period of Dio and Herodian.

We can then add two key later Roman sources, Ammianus Marcellinus with his *Later Roman History*, and Publius Vegetius Renatus with his *Epitome of Military Science*. The former provides great insight into Roman special operations given he himself was a leading member of the *protectores* considered in Chapter 5, his exploits alongside the *magister equitum*

Ursicinus illuminating a life of derring-do in imperial service. Meanwhile, the latter's work later became a crucial textbook for Renaissance military commanders and is particularly useful when considering Roman special operations given the detail it provides to counter specific threats such as guerrilla warfare (see below). Next with regard to later Roman sources, we can also add the works of the Latin chroniclers Flavius Eutropius, Aurelius Victor, Jerome and Paulus Orosius. The first three (and given their use as sources by the fourth, that too by default) likely used as a major source, the so-called 'Kaisergeschichte' hypothetical set of short histories now lost. Finally in terms of primary sources, we have contemporary or later itineraries and lists. These include the *Tabula Peutingeriana*, *Antonine Itinerary*, *Ravenna Cosmography* and *Notitia Dignitatum*, the latter a key list of late Roman military offices across the empire and so particularly important.

In terms of modern sources, in the first instance this has included my own academic research over the last sixteen years through my MA in War Studies from KCL, MA in Archaeology from UCL and PhD in Classics and Archaeology from the University of Kent. Additionally, my recently published works on Roman themes have proved a fertile source of new information on Roman special forces. These include *Sea Eagles of Empire: The Classis Britannica and the Battles for Britain*, *Empire State: How the Roman Military Built an Empire*, *Septimius Severus in Scotland: The Northern Campaigns of the First Hammer of the Scots*, *Roman Legionaries*, *Pertinax: The Son of a Slave Who Became Roman Emperor*, *Romans at War*, *Roman Britain's Missing Legion: What Really Happened to legio IX Hispana?* and *Roman Conquests: Britain*.

Meanwhile, as core modern references with a general focus on the Roman military, the many works of Adrian Goldsworthy and Ross Cowan have provided much of the vivid detail needed when considering the daily lives of Roman troops of all types. Additionally, Tim Cornell and John Matthews' *Atlas of the Roman World* has provided much of the key geographical background when detailing the many campaigning theatres where the Romans employed special forces. Next, when looking specifically at Roman Britain for examples of special force activity, David Mattingly's *An Imperial Possession: Britain in the Roman Empire* has proved invaluable, as has Patricia Southern's *Roman Britain* and Sam Moorhead and David Stuttard's *The Romans Who Shaped Britain*. Meanwhile, with regard to works with a focus on Roman interests in Scotland (again the setting for much special forces activity), I have found Andrew Tibbs' *Beyond the Empire*, David Breeze's *Roman Scotland*, Lawrence Keppie's *The Legacy of Rome* and Anthony Kamm's *The Last Frontier* most useful.

Moving on to special operations in the modern world, key sources have included James D. Kiras' *Special Operations and Strategy: From World War II to the War on Terrorism*, Harry S. Brown's *The Command and Control of Special Operations Forces* and William H. McRaven's *Spec Ops: Case Studies in Special Operations Warfare Theory and Practice*. When looking at first person accounts of such special operations, I have also used a variety of memoirs including Otto Skorzeny's *Special Missions* and Viktor Suvorov's *Spetsnaz: The Inside Story of the Soviet Special Forces*.

When our focus turns specifically to Roman special forces, we are then fortunate that a variety of sound academic texts are available to guide the research. In long form these include Norman Austin and Boris Rankov's *Exploratio: Military and Political Intelligence in the Roman World from the Second Punic War to the Battle of Adrianople*, Rose Mary Sheldon's *Intelligence Activities in Ancient Rome* and Jakub Grygiel's *Return of the Barbarians: Confronting Non-State Actors from Ancient Rome to the Present*. Shorter papers referenced include Adam Leong Kok Wey's *Western and Eastern Ways of Special Warfare*, Ross Cowan's *Exploratores*, Kathryn Langenfeld's *Imperial Spies and Intercepted letters in the Late Roman Empire* and *Forged Letters and Court Intrigue in the Reign of Constantius II*, Naco del Hoyo's *Roman and Pontic Intelligence Strategies: Politics and War in the Time of Mithradates VI*, and William Sinnigen's *Two Branches of the Late Roman Secret Service* and *The Roman Secret Service*.

Next some housekeeping notes, starting with key definitions:

- *Special Operations and Special Forces*. Given their central role in this book these terms deserve consideration in their own chapter, and so are covered in depth in Chapter 1. Note that in the modern world units engaged in special operations are also called special operations forces (SOF), but to avoid confusion here given the focus on the ancient world (and the multitude of troop types considered) I keep the two terms separate.
- *Elite*. A more complicated word than it needs to be in this book given in public use it can reference both higher quality mainstream military

units (for example guard troops) and also special forces. Therefore, at each use here I endeavour to ensure the reader is aware which is being referenced.
- *Symmetric and Asymmetric Warfare.* War between fairly evenly matched belligerents, or conflict where one is so dominant that the other is forced to use unconventional strategies and tactics, for example guerilla warfare. By way of example, in the Roman world their many conflicts with the Sassanid Persians can be described as symmetrical given both sides were so evenly matched, while their campaigns against the natives in the far north of Britain often forced the latter to respond asymmetrically.
- *Guerilla Warfare.* Irregular warfare fought by asymmetrically inferior combatants using unconventional tactics.
- *Commando.* A commonly used term for elite soldiers (of both kinds, see above) carrying out special operations. The name is derived from the Latin *commandare*, meaning to command. In a modern context it first came into use through the Dutch word 'Kommando' used to describe the highly mobile Boer mounted infantry columns which proved so effective in the First Boer War (1880–1881). Soon its use was so widespread that a unit of such irregulars came to be called a commando.
- *Annihilation.* The complete destruction of an enemy through winning a decisive engagement over its armed forces.
- *Attrition.* A more prolonged form of conflict that gradually wears down an opponent over time, sometimes called Strategic Attrition.
- *Strategic Paralysis.* A theory based on the complete defeat of an opponent using methods which minimize cost in terms of manpower and material, often through the use of innovative technology or tactics. Kiras (2006, 13) describes this as 'the delivery of a crippling moral blow that makes extended material struggle unnecessary.' Strategic paralysis is often considered an extension of the annihilation route to military success, rather than through the use of attrition.
- *Relative Superiority.* A crucial concept behind successful special operations activity. McRaven (1995, 4) describes this as 'a condition that exists when an attacking force, generally smaller, gains a decisive advantage over a larger or well defended enemy.'

- *The Roman Republic and Empire.* The activities of Roman special forces covered in this book fit broadly into three time periods. These are the Roman Republic, and the Principate and Dominate phases of the Roman Empire.

  The first began in 509 BC with the overthrow of the last Etrusco-Roman king Tarquin the Proud. It ended, and the Principate Empire began, following the Senate's acclamation of Augustus as the first emperor in 27 BC. The name is derived from the term *princeps* (chief or master), referencing the emperor as the leading citizen of the empire. This phase lasted until AD 284 with the accession of Diocletian. Faced with dragging the empire out of the disastrous 'Crisis of the Third Century', he instituted a series of structural changes that altered the very nature of the Roman world. This featured a new, far more overtly imperial system of government that set the emperor up as something more akin to an eastern potentate. The name of this last phase of empire, the Dominate, is based on the word *dominus*, referencing lord or master.

- *Legionaries and Auxiliaries.* For the majority of the Roman Republic, and the Principate phase of empire, the premier Roman warrior was the legionary, a heavily armed and armoured infantryman who most often formed the main line of battle. From the time of Augustus, supporting troops were then organized into formal units known as auxiliaries, often lesser in quality to the legionaries but still a match for most opponents the Romans faced. Auxiliaries provided both foot troops and most of the cavalry in Roman imperial armies. Later, a blurring took place in the quality of legionaries and auxilia foot troops, and as the Dominate phase of empire progressed a new type of auxiliary emerged to replace the legionaries as the troop type of choice for Roman commanders. These were the *auxilia palatina*, first raised by Constantine I to help bolster the legions in his field armies. In this later period the Roman state also began to recruit large numbers of mercenaries who fought in their native style, at first under Roman officers and later their own leaders. These were called *foederates*.

Moving on to other housekeeping matters, Roman military installations play a key role in this book given they were the bases from which special operations were mounted. In that regard I have used the current size-based hierarchy as a means of describing their size as they occur in the narrative. Starting with the largest, these are 20 ha-plus legionary fortresses for one or more legions, then 12 ha-plus vexillation fortresses holding a mixed force of legionary cohorts and auxiliaries, next one ha-plus forts for outpost garrisons, and finally fortlets for a small auxiliary unit. Military settlements associated with such fortifications are called a *canaba* when connected with a legionary fortress, and a *vicus* elsewhere.

Finally in terms of housekeeping, with regard to the use of classical and modern place names I have (usually) used the modern name, referencing its Roman name at the first point of use in the main text if it is known. Meanwhile, where a classical name for a role, position or event is well understood I use that, referencing the modern name or term at the first use. Additionally, when emperors are first detailed in the main narrative I have listed the dates of their reign where appropriate.

Lastly, here I would like to thank the many people who have helped make this work on Roman special forces possible. As always this includes Dr Andrew Gardner at UCL's Institute of Archaeology, Dr Steve Willis at the University of Kent and Professor Andrew Lambert of the War Studies Department at KCL. The latter in particular has kindly guided me when researching special forces in the modern world. Next my publisher Phil Sidnell, the inspiration behind this book. Also Dr John Lambshead for his kind help with regard to ancient sources regarding special force operations. Then my patient proofreader and lovely wife Sara, and my dad John Elliott and friend Francis Tusa, both companions in my various escapades to research this book. As with all of my literary work, all have contributed greatly and freely, enabling this work on Roman special forces to reach fruition. Finally, I would like to thank my family, especially my tolerant wife Sara once again and children Alex (also a student of military history) and Lizzie.

Thank you all.
Simon Elliott
February 2023

Chapter 1

What Are Special Operations and Special Forces?

Before we consider special operations and special forces in the ancient world, we first have to define what they are. I do that at the beginning of this chapter, where I then set out a series of criteria to enable the ancient world examples to be considered. To provide background, here I also briefly detail a short history of modern special operations and special forces. Note this is not a comprehensive review, but simply to provide further context for the ancient world examples in later chapters.

Defining Special Operations and Special Forces

What are special operations and special forces? Defining them today is problematic given misuse of the terms over the past century by politicians and military leaders who have often viewed their use as a low cost, surgical alternative to more expensive and wider military engagement (certainly in the west). Some commentators have gone further here, for example Gray who argues some decision takers have viewed them as a 'free lunch' when faced with difficult foreign policy decisions (1998, 155).

Starting with special operations, these sit within the wider context of the strategy being utilized in a given military context. Thus, far from special operations alone leading to the singular defeat of an opponent, they are more often than not actually part of the wider military engagement. As Kiras says (2006, 3): 'Although special operations are useful tactically in the whittling away of adversary material resources, their strategic impact will be negligible if this is the only purpose for which they are used.'

Therefore, in my view special operations more frequently err towards making an attritional contribution to victory rather than securing military success through an annihilation strategy (though noting others have the opposite view).

What special operations can do is inflict disproportionate material and moral damage on an enemy, especially given their unique ability to accomplish military tasks thought impossible. This allows a tighter definition of special operations, useful later when considering Roman special forces, and here I turn to Luttwak, Canby and Thomas who argued they are 'self contained acts of war mounted by self-sufficient forces within hostile territory' (1982, 30), whose actions still sit within wider military strategy.

Defining special operations, and understanding their use, then allows special forces to be characterized. In this regard Leong Kok Wey is helpful, he explaining that (2019, 144):

> There are numerous definitions of special operations. These…can be divided into two categories: one based on a rigid assumption that special operations are what a special forces unit does, and the second on a broader definition of what a special operation is and a suggestion of who should conduct it.

Thus in the first and narrow instance special operations are only conducted by special forces, and in the second and broader instance they are conducted by whatever package of forces are required, including special forces but also other troop types. To my mind the latter unhelpfully widens those engaged in special operations too far, for example in a modern context to include transport assets. I think that is distracting in our consideration of special forces in the Roman world, and therefore I opt for the former, with special operations being only those carried out by special forces. That also allows one to discount other elite forces within the normal military framework from consideration in the core text of the book, for example in a Roman context Praetorians and other guard units (though noting these are detailed in Chapter 2 by way of background).

We can now consider what such special forces actually do. First, picking up the earlier arguments that special forces don't operate in isolation from wider military activity, Brown argues in his wide-ranging review of the command and control of special forces in the 1991 Gulf War that (1996, v):

Today integrated operations are a prime requirement of special forces and general purpose forces of all services. None can unilaterally conduct operations because of strategic lift and logistic limitations. No unit is capable of all types of missions nor should any unit or its leadership believe it is capable of all types of missions.

Nevertheless, special forces both in the Roman world and today are different from mainstream armed forces, and here I first turn to the US military for its definition to guide us. In its official Doctrine for Joint Operations it specifically describes special operations carried out by special forces as activities in hostile, denied or politically sensitive environments to achieve military, diplomatic, informational and economic objectives which employ military capabilities for which there is no conventional force option. More broadly, current NATO doctrine defines special operations and special forces as 'military activities conducted by specially designated, organized, trained, and equipped forces, manned with selected personnel, using unconventional tactics, techniques, and modes of employment.' Meanwhile, in describing the activities of the Spetsnaz (a broad term for the special forces of the Soviet Union, and later those of Russia and the various Soviet successor states) Galeotti is even more specific. He says that traditionally they are primarily deployed in battlefield reconnaissance roles deep in enemy territory, and are additionally tasked with shattering enemy chains of command, disrupting lines of supply and targeting (in a Cold War context) NATO nuclear weapons (2015, 5).

From such descriptions we can put in place a set of criteria by which to measure whether the various manifestations of Roman special operations are akin to modern special forces, or not. I determine that these criteria are:

- Special forces comprise elite volunteers who are chosen through a demanding selection process.
- Special forces are uniquely trained for non-regular warfare, with special skill sets, a bespoke *esprit de corps* and access to specialist equipment.
- Special forces are used to secure operational and strategic advantage, rather than for normal military operations. This might for example include attacking hostile leaders and strategic assets deep in enemy

territory. Therefore, they are not merely elite combat units fielded in the normal line of battle.
- When required, the use of special forces is totally deniable.

I will use a balance of the above four criteria at the end of each following chapter in a Closing Discussion to determine whether the Roman 'special forces' detailed in each would today be called such.

Special Operations and Special Forces in the Modern World

Based on the above criteria, the first military units in the modern world that might be considered 'special' date to the mid-nineteenth century. These were irregular units deployed by the British Indian Army to help secure the north-western frontier in colonial India. This was a fluid combat environment where competing British and Russian foreign policy interests in Afghanistan and the Punjab continually destabilized the border region.

The first such unit was the Corps of Guides, created by the British soldier statesman Sir Henry Lawrence. By 1845 he had become the political advisor to Henry Hardinge, colonial governor general in India. Lawrence then played a key role in bringing the First Anglo-Sikh War to an end in the Punjab in 1846. Recognizing the need to have reliable eyes and ears in this frontier zone he then founded the Guides, with Lieutenant Harry Lumsden its first commander. The force had modest beginnings, comprising only one company of cavalry and two of infantry when it first gathered at its new base at Kalu Khan in the Peshawar Valley. It then tripled in size to participate in the Second Anglo-Sikh War (1848–1849), where it specialized in irregular operations behind enemy lines, before playing a key role in the Indian Mutiny when it gained fame by marching 600 miles in three weeks in mid-summer to participate in the siege of Delhi. After the formalization of British military forces in India following the suppression of the mutiny the Guides were incorporated into the new Frontier Force Brigade, though maintained their independence. Around this time they also became the first unit in the British army to wear khaki as opposed to brightly-coloured uniforms. The Guides then remained in British Indian Army service through to the partition of India in 1947, following the withdrawal of British colonial rule.

The second specialist irregular unit created by the British in India were the Gurkha Scouts. This was formed in the early 1890s, again to operate in the north-west frontier zone where it carried out special operations against opponents of the British regime to the south. It was first used at full strength in the 1897–1898 Tirah Campaign against the native Afridi tribe in the Khyber Pass region. As with the Guides, the Gurkha Scouts continued in use through to the partition.

The development of 'special' forces continued in the context of the British imperial experience, next in the Second Boer War. This was a particularly brutal conflict lasting from 1899 to 1902, where the empire's regular forces struggled to get to grips with their Boer opponents who fought a highly successful asymmetrical campaign against an opponent far superior in numbers. This not only led to a change in the battlefield tactics of the British, including the widespread adoption of khaki uniforms, but also the creation of new and bespoke 'special' units. As with India, these had their origins in a requirement to provide an improved scouting function, with troops able to operate behind enemy lines in terrain well-known to their opponents. The best-known are the Lovat Scouts, founded in 1900 by Simon Fraser, the 14th Lord Lovat. He recruited his new regiment entirely from Scottish Highland gamekeepers who wore their ghillie suits and were renowned for their marksmanship. In keeping with later 'special' units the Lovat Scouts reported directly to Lord Roberts, the British commander in the conflict, through his Chief of Scouts Major Frederick Russell Burnham. The unit, which later became the Sharpshooters, was eventually incorporated into the regular British Army. Other irregular British units deployed in South Africa at the time included the Bushveldt Carbineers, later called the Pietersburg Light Horse. This unit was formed in February 1901 and saw extensive action in the Northern Transvaal.

The advent of the First World War saw the use of 'special' units evolve even further, with for example German Stormtroopers and Italian Arditi among the first specialist shock troops of the industrial age. Here they competed with new 'special' game changing technologies, for example aircraft and, following its British innovation, the tank. Both had exponents who claimed they were the vector by which strategic paralysis could be achieved against the enemy, and so victory. In the event though, the evolution of combined operations by the allies at the end of the conflict proved the most successful means of achieving success, at least on the battlefield. Meanwhile 'special' operations were also carried out on a greater scale in this conflict than any previously, for example the Zeebrugge Raid in April 1918 when a British combined arms force under Royal Navy command attempted to block the key Belgian port of Brugge-Zeebrugge. However, it was in the Second World War that the use of special forces in the modern sense truly came of age, as I now detail.

Special Forces and the Second World War
All protagonists in the Second World War used 'special' military units of various kinds to carry out special operations, which as the conflict progressed evolved into what we today would call special forces based on the criteria set out at the beginning of this chapter. Here they are considered country by country.

In Britain, the British Commandos were formed in 1940. This was in the context of Germany's on-going military successes on the continent. Keen to take the fight to the occupied territories there, and with France on the verge of falling, the Prime Minister Winston Churchill called for a new ruthless approach to the conflict, saying that 'Enterprises must be prepared, with specially-trained troops of the hunter class, who can develop a reign of terror down these coasts, first of all on the butcher and bolt policy' (Haskew, 2007, 47). Here he was fortunate given a freethinking staff officer named Lieutenant Colonel Dudley Clarke had already prepared and submitted a proposal to Britain's Chief of the Imperial General Staff, Sir John Dill. This was for a cadre of specially selected troops, highly motivated and skilled in demolition techniques, to be deployed by small vessels to attack coastal installations. With Churchill's backing Dill approved the plan, after which things moved forward quickly, with the first commando raid taking place on the 24 June 1940. This was against German installations south of Boulogne-sur-Mer (notably given the book's focus a Roman founding, then called *Gessoriacum*) and Le Touquet. At this point the new force was called No 11 Independent Company.

By late 1940 more than 2,000 men had volunteered to join the new unit, which proved a huge draw for those seeking active service taking the fight to the enemy in German-occupied Europe. Here, Kiras says

(2006, 87): 'There was no shortage of volunteers for individuals looking to exchange the tedium of barrack life and manoeuvres for dangerous action.'

By November the new force was being called the Special Service Brigade. This initially consisted of four battalions commanded by Brigadier J.C. Haydon, though this structure proved cumbersome for special operations where nimble formations were needed for the surgical operations being planned. The brigade's structure was therefore radically changed, and now comprised twelve independent units, each called a commando for the first time and individually numbered. The commandos featured 450 men, with a lieutenant colonel in command of each.

Recruitment into this elite volunteer force was very strict, as McRaven details (1995, 118):

> All trainees went through a 12-week basic selection course. This training included cliff assaults, close-quarter combat with rifles, knives, and garrottes, assault courses, survival training, river crossings, and live-fire exercises. Strong emphasis was placed both on perfecting amphibious raiding skills and on having the confidence and initiative to use those skills when confronted with a difficult situation.

Such was the success of the commando initiative in Europe, at least from a morale perspective, that by the year's end a depot had been set up to expand their operations to the Middle East. Then, in February 1942, Haydon established a full-time training headquarters at Achnacarry in the Scottish Highlands under the command of Lieutenant Colonel Charles Vaughan. This introduced a new, even tougher training regime based on operational experience. Realism was the key here, with a particular focus on discipline under fire, and it is noteworthy that during the war over forty commando candidates were killed while training at Achnacarry, most in live fire exercises (McRaven, 1995, 119). Commando training also emphasized the need for teamwork, with candidates encouraged to operate in pairs to overcome obstacles.

Soon the commandos had reached their full wartime strength with over thirty units of various sizes, including four full assault brigades. They were to participate in all of the major campaigns in the conflict, sometimes leading as with the Operation Chariot raid on St Nazaire in March 1942 when Number 2 Commando supplied most of the troops, and sometimes supporting as with the Operation Overlord Normandy landings in June 1944. Eventually the commandos were to serve in all theatres of the conflict, ranging from the Arctic Circle to South East Asia. After the war their success was then replicated in the new elite forces set up by Britain's European allies, with examples including the French Commandos Marine, Belgian Paracommando Brigade and Dutch Korps Commandotroepen. These all had a direct association with their British progenitor given they were formed from former members of Britain's No 10 Commando, whose recruits all came from occupied Europe.

The commandos also formed the basis of other British units that carried out special operations during the war. A prime example would be Colonel Orde Wingate's 'Chindits', an irregular force that performed long-range penetrations deep behind Japanese lines in Burma to disrupt communications and interdict troops' movements. This comprised troops seconded from the commandos together with infantry recruited from the King's Regiment (Liverpool) and Ghurkhas.

However, it was another unit with origins with the commandos that many argue was the first example of a modern special force. This was the iconic Special Air Service (SAS), founded in July 1941 by Lieutenant David Stirling. Earlier, in June 1940 he had volunteered to join No 8 (Guards) Commando in the Middle East. This unit was part of Layforce, an ad hoc formation of 2,000 men from various commando units under the command of Colonel Robert Laycock. This was tasked with carrying out deep penetration raids in the desert to disrupt enemy lines of communications in the eastern Mediterranean. However, given the precarious British position in the region once the Germans arrived in theatre to support the Italians, Layforce soon found itself used as a theatre reserve, with elements fighting in Bardia, Crete, Syria and Tobruk. Eventually the force was disbanded in August 1941.

However, Stirling was impressed with Laycock's ideas while serving under him. He remained convinced that a small team of highly trained and motivated troops could create more damage to the enemy's ability to fight than a whole platoon if it maintained the element of surprise. Specifically, he developed a concept whereby small groups of parachute-trained troops would operate behind enemy lines, gaining intelligence, attacking supply routes and destroying aircraft on the ground at airfields which were often remote, especially in the desert.

To take his plan forward he orchestrated a meeting with General Claude Auchinleck, the commander of British forces in the Middle East. The latter was impressed and relayed Stirling's ideas to London where the military high command endorsed the creation of a new unit comprising five officers and sixty troopers. This gathered at Kabrit Camp in Egypt on the River Nile where it was disingenuously named L Detachment, Special Air Service Brigade. The idea here was to convince the Germans and Italians that it was a new brigade of paratroopers when, in reality, Stirling's original force was more a motorized flying column. Its early missions proved highly successful, particularly when working in conjunction with the existing Long Range Desert Group (LRDG), an elite unit already tasked with deep penetration behind enemy lines in the desert, though on a larger scale.

By early 1942 the SAS was undertaking increasingly ambitious operations, for example the raid on the Libyan village of Bouerat, a key German and Italian logistics base. Here severe damage was done to the harbour, petrol tanks and storage facilities on the coast. Later, a raid on Benghazi damaged fifteen aircraft at the nearby airfield of Al-Berka. Then in July, Stirling himself personally led a deep combined SAS/ LRDG raid on the German airfields at Fuka and Mersa Matruh where thirty aircraft were destroyed. Here you can see special operations begin to have a significant impact on the enemy's ability to fight effectively, and this in the period before the turn of allied fortunes at the Battle of El Alamein in October that year. Thus, these SAS and LRDG operations in early and mid-1942 were a key component of the allied strategy of taking the fight back to an enemy.

The SAS continued to play an important role throughout the rest of the North African campaign, also operating in the Greek islands and later featuring in the invasions of Sicily and Italy. The majority of its troops then returned to the UK where they were formed into a brigade with two British, two French and one Belgian regiment, these all going on to conduct operations in France, the Low Countries and finally Germany as the war came to a close. Here Kiras (2006, 14) makes an interesting observation about the difficulty in scaling up such embryonic special force activities when tasked with playing a wider role in overall allied strategy on the continent. Specifically highlighting the role of the SAS in the campaign against the German 7th Army in the immediate aftermath of the Normandy landings in June 1944, he says:

> Competing interests, the rapid expansion of the SAS, dysfunctional command arrangements, political constraints, friction, and German adaption ensured that the SAS played a marginal role in eroding German morale or material reserves. Instead of focusing on a phased effort designed to disrupt the 7th Army's lifeline to Germany…SAS teams were instead scattered throughout France to conduct tactical attrition of German reserves and rear area security units.

In this case the SAS, easily capable of playing a far more important role in destroying the fighting capability of the 7th Army and thus speeding the collapse of German resistance in France, instead found itself widely dispersed and so less effective in a strategic sense. In particular, it suffered from the British Special Operations Executive's (SOE) desire to continue its leading role in planning and controlling special operations behind enemy lines in Europe. However, despite this setback, lessons were learned and by the end of the war the SAS was again playing a decisive role within wider allied strategy. Note should also be made here of the Special Boat Service (SBS) which was similarly formed during the Second World War, in this instance to carry out bespoke maritime special operations, a task in which it excelled.

Britain was not the only nation to develop a significant special operations capability in the Second World War. For example, in the United States the Office of Strategic Services (OSS) was established in June 1942 by Presidential Order as an agency of the Joint Chiefs of Staff. This wide ranging organization was tasked with intelligence gathering, special operations behind enemy lines, training insurgents willing to fight the Axis powers in occupied territories, propaganda and subversion, and post-war planning. It was dissolved a month after the end of the war, with its intelligence gathering responsibilities later resumed by the Central Intelligence Agency (CIA).

The United States armed forces also featured a number of other specialist military formations, often specifically linked to its various service branches. For example the Marine Raiders unit was formed in February

1942 as an elite battalion with the specific aim of securing beachheads in amphibious operations. Meanwhile, the United States Army Rangers was formed in June 1942 after Major-General Lucian Truscott (a liaison officer with the British General Staff) made a proposal that the United States form a unit along the lines of the British Commandos.

In Germany, the Brandenburg Regiment was established by Captain Theodor von Hippel as an extension of the Abwehr military's intelligence agency. Recruits were sourced from all branches of the German military, with German-speaking foreign nationals particularly favoured. The service fought in all theatres during the Second World War, with a particular specialization the seizing of operationally important targets through infiltration and sabotage.

The Waffen SS (the combat branch of the Nazi Party's SS organisation) also set up its own special operations unit, most likely as a counter to the Brandenburg Regiment given the latter's successes early in the war. This was initially called the SS Sonderverband z.b.V. Friedenthal, later being renamed the 502nd SS Jagdverband 502. Its most famous commander was Austrian-born Otto Skorzeny who led it on some of its most notable missions. These included the Operation Oak glider-borne assault to rescue the Italian dictator Benito Mussolini in September 1943, and the infamous Operation Griffin false-flag mission aimed at sowing disorder behind the allied lines during Operation Wacht Am Rhein, the late 1944 Ardennes Offensive.

Skorzeny's extensive memoires are very insightful when studying the mindset of those engaged in special operations, especially when considering the risk-reward balance, this often much further skewed towards the former compared to standard military operations. For example, he goes into great detail about the planning for the Mussolini rescue operation. Here, the former Italian dictator was being held at the Campo Imperatore Hotel in a ski resort in Italy's Gran Sasso massif high in the Apennine Mountains. As Skorzeny explains (1950, 71):

> A ground operation seemed hopeless from the start. An attack up the steep rocky slopes would have cost us very heavy losses, apart from giving good notice to the enemy and leaving them time to conceal their prisoner...So a ground operation was ruled out. The

factor of surprise could be our only trump card…so a glider landing remained the only solution.

Skorzeny also reflects on the *esprit de corps* experienced by those engaged in special operations, for example speaking of his delight at being interrogated while incarcerated in Nuremberg after the war by Major General William Donovan, head of the OSS (1950, 206). Skorzeny clearly felt they were both set well apart from the normal rank and file military.

Other Axis powers also formed bespoke units to carry out special operations, for example Italy's Decima Flottiglia MAS frogman unit of the Regia Marina Navy which carried out a number of high profile attacks on British shipping in major ports around the Mediterranean. The most notable was the December 1941 raid on Alexandria when six frogmen used manned torpedoes to plant limpet mines which badly damaged the battleships HMS *Valiant* and HMS *Queen Elizabeth*. The Italian air force also formed the Arditi Distruttori Regia Aeronautica raiding force during the war. This performed deep penetration missions in the North Africa desert in a similar manner to the British LRDG. On one notable occasion the unit destroyed 25 US Army Air Force (USAAF) Consolidated B-24 Liberator heavy bombers in a raid on an allied airfield. Meanwhile Japan also fielded a number of special operations units, for example the army's 2nd Raiding Brigade, known as the Takachiho Paratroopers.

As can be seen, the Second World War featured a proliferation of special operations units, and by the end of the war some could accurately be termed special forces as we would describe them today. The prime example would be the SAS, though note should be taken of the original role played by the British Commandos in many of the units detailed above.

Special Forces Today
In the latter half of the twentieth century units carrying out special operations proliferated as political and military leaders became increasingly aware of their ability to deliver clandestine (and often anonymous, at least in terms of the individuals involved) foreign policy and defence outcomes. Such units then entered the wider public's consciousness through a series of high profile operations, for example the 1976 Israeli raid on Entebbe and the 1980 SAS Iranian Embassy siege assault in London. Both are

worthy of short consideration here given they illustrate how special forces have come to be used today.

The Israeli special operation to rescue the hostages in Entebbe, Uganda was called Operation Jonathan. It began with the hijacking of Air France flight AF 139 on Sunday, 27 June 1976 while en route from Lod Airport in Israel to Paris. The Airbus A300 had just departed Athens on a refuelling stop when the 254 passengers were taken hostage by two German nationals from the radical left Baader-Meinhof Gang, and two Palestinians from the Palestinian Liberation Organisation (PLO). The Israeli government immediately placed its Sayeret Matkal counter-terrorist unit (colloquially known as Unit) on alert.

Initially Yitzhak Rabin's Israeli government thought the hijackers planned to return the aircraft to Lod, as had happened in previous hijackings. There they could get maximum publicity for their cause. Unit therefore began planning its rescue operation with that assumption in mind. However, instead the Airbus landed at Benghazi in Libya, and later headed for Entebbe. The hijackers then released all but 106 of the captives, the latter all Israeli, non-Israeli Jewish or members of the Air France air crew who all refused repatriation. They then issued demands for the release of fifty-three militants imprisoned in West Germany, Kenya, Israel and elsewhere, saying that if these demands were not met then they would begin executing the remaining captives. A stand-off soon developed, giving the Israeli government time to formulate a response. Initially it was hoped to avoid bloodshed through the intervention of the Ugandan President Idi Amin. However, it quickly became clear that he was favouring the kidnappers. Therefore, planning for a military special operation to rescue the captives began in earnest (McRaven, 1995, 336).

Initially a maritime operation on Lake Victoria was considered given Entebbe and its airport are located on a peninsula on the Ugandan side of this vast body of water. This mission was due to be led by Israeli marines in rubber boats, but the operation was soon ruled out when training revealed the inflatables, due to be air dropped, burst on impact with the water. This left only the extremely high-risk option of an aerial assault.

The airborne rescue was launched on 3 July when four Israeli Air Force (IAF) Lockheed C-130H Hercules transport aircraft took off for Entebbe. They carried 200 troops between them, led by a 29-man Unit assault force, together with armoured personnel carriers. The four transports were escorted by newly delivered IAF McDonnell Douglas F-4E Phantom jet fighters. Additionally, two Boeing 707s joined the mission, one as the command aircraft and one an aerial hospital.

After flying over 4,000 km from Israel to Uganda involving multiple air-to-air refuellings, the Israeli force staged a remarkable *coup de main*, with the hostages rescued within an hour of the first Hercules landing. All of the militants, by then numbering seven, were killed, and eleven Ugandan Air Force MiG 21 fighters destroyed to prevent any aerial pursuit of the returning aircraft. The Israelis lost one soldier in the operation, notably Lieutenant Colonel Yonatan Netanyahu who was the Unit assault force commander, while three hostages and a number of Ugandan soldiers were also killed. On the return trip, the Israeli aircraft met the waiting hospital aircraft in the Kenyan capital Nairobi where all refuelled before returning to Israel.

The Israeli raid on Entebbe is remarkable for a number reasons, most notably as a supreme example of the application of relative superiority. It is also highly insightful when looking at how special operations are planned. As McRaven (1995, 367) says:

> With less than two days to plan and prepare a major assault mission, the Israelis developed the simplest option for success. During the planning phase, they limited their objectives, used intelligence to identify the obstacles, and then applied technology and innovation to overcome the obstacles. During the preparation phase...the units involved conducted several partial and full-scale rehearsals. During the execution phase, the Israelis gained surprise by using boldness and deception to momentarily confuse the Ugandans, and (then) by moving quickly on the target they were able to secure the hostages within three minutes of landing at Entebbe.

Operation Jonathan is thus an excellent example of a modern special forces-led operation, though event deniability wasn't an option here given the high profile nature of the hijacking, and desire on the part of the Israeli government to deter future such events.

While the Israeli raid on Entebbe was a high profile event, the SAS Iranian Embassy rescue operation went one better. This was because Operation Nimrod was shown on live television, effectively announcing the existence of modern special forces to the wider public. Matters began on 30 April 1980 when a group of six Iranian terrorists stormed the embassy on Prince's Gate, South Kensington in London. There they took twenty-six people hostage, including the embassy staff, several visiting bystanders and a police officer who was there guarding the embassy. The assault took British security services by surprise given the hostage-takers were from an obscure terrorist organization who opposed the new Iranian regime of Ayatollah Khomeini, they demanding the release of prisoners who had been campaigning for the autonomy of the oil-rich province of Khuzestan Province in south-western Iran.

There then followed the famous five-day siege, with the SAS finally authorized to begin their rescue on 5 May after the murder of a hostage, and the belief another may have been killed. This involved the spectacular televised breaching of the embassy building by two teams of abseiling SAS troopers attacking in waves. The raid lasted just seventeen minutes and involved thirty-five soldiers. During the action, the terrorists killed another hostage and seriously wounded two others, while the SAS killed all but one of the hostage-takers. The rescued hostages and the remaining terrorist, still hiding among them, were then taken to the embassy's back garden where the last terrorist was identified. Once again event deniability wasn't an option here given the presence of the media.

Notably, both of these examples featured special-forces-led operations in non-conflict situations. We can turn to more recent examples to show special forces operating in wider conflicts, for example the 1982 Falklands War where both the SAS and SBS played prominent roles, this further securing British special forces in the public consciousness. Deniability is interesting in this conflict, with the vast majority of actions by the two services publicly unrecorded, though with some high profile examples being heavily publicized to boost campaign morale and undermine that of their Argentinian opponents. The raid on Pebble Island is one such case, where British special forces destroyed six FMA IA58 Pucara ground-attack aircraft, four Turbo Mentor light aircraft and a Short's Skyvan light-transport aircraft on the night of 14 May.

More recently, special forces have played key roles in the various engagements in Afghanistan over the past four decades, in both Gulf Wars in 1991 and 2003, and in the ongoing campaigns in the Middle East against both Al-Qaeda and Islamic State. In the first, Soviet and later Russian Spetsnaz first came to public prominence, while US special forces emerged publicly for the first time, with for example the US Navy SEALs and the US Army's 1st Special Forces Operational Detachment–Delta (better known as Delta Force) prominent in their activities.

Through to today, special forces continue to be a key instrument for many nations in the implementation of their foreign and defence policies, to the extent that often there is a public expectation that they will be used even when normal military activities will suffice.

Of course, special operations and special forces are not a new phenomenon, even in the modern contexts set out above. As Reiters argues 'Special operations and the forces that conduct them are not exclusively a modern concern' (2021, 17). With that in mind, I now turn back to the ancient world to begin my review of such activity there.

Chapter 2

Specialist and Elite Roman Troops

As with all armies, those of the Roman Republic and Roman Empire featured specialist troop types, and also elite warriors who often provided the guard troops for senior leaders. In terms of the latter, the best-known are the Praetorian Guards of the Principate Roman emperors.

Examining such troops, even when clearly not special forces set against the criteria detailed in Chapter 1, is still useful as it sets a benchmark by which to judge the true special force candidates considered in later chapters. Therefore, here I consider a variety of specialist Roman troop types, before next examining Roman elite units. First though, the chapter begins with a brief summary of the key time periods within the Roman Republic, and Principate and Dominate phases of empire. This is designed to provide a chronological template to guide the reader as the wider narrative on Roman special forces unfolds.

Republic and Empire

Key aspects of the Roman world differed greatly in its Republican, Principate and Dominate phases of existence. These are now considered in chronological order.

The Roman Republic
This began in 509 BC after Tarquin the Proud, last of the Etrusco-Roman kings, was overthrown (Holland, 2003, 2). It comprised three broad time periods:

- The early Republican period when Rome, a fairly unremarkable Latin town on the eastern banks of the River Tiber, began to expand its influence at the expense of neighbouring city-states and cultures. Its first opponents were the Etruscans to the north, and the various hill tribes to the east in the Apennine Mountains. It was also during this period that Rome was famously sacked in 390 BC by the Senones Gauls under their king Brennus, after the hoplite-based early Roman army had been crushed at the Battle of Allia. One result of these twin-disasters was the building of the Servian Wall circuit around Rome, the town's first physical defensive structure. Another was the military reformation of the great warrior statesman Marcus Furius Camillus who introduced the maniple-based legion for the first time, this comprising three classes of heavy infantry. These were the *triarii* veterans, *principes* older warriors and *hastati* 'flower of the young men' (Elliott, 31, 2018b).

- The middle Republican period when Rome first came to dominate the Italian peninsula, initially defeating its key regional rivals including the Samnites. Then later, as Rome expanded its influence across the western Mediterranean, it fought three sanguineous conflicts against the Carthaginian Empire. Concurrently, engagement with the Hellenistic world in the eastern Mediterranean also inevitably led to conflict with the Macedonian kingdom, Greek city states, Seleucid Empire, the Parthians and Ptolemaic Egypt. By the middle of the second century BC the power of the Roman military had carried all before it, with Rome the dominant power across the entire Mediterranean, or *mare nostrum* as the Romans came to know it. In this outlandish achievement the Romans showed the two key traits that came to define its ability to thrive and prosper, even in great adversity. The first was true grit, the ability to come back from the most fearsome losses and ultimately win a conflict. The second was the skill with which the Romans adopted and adapted the military tactics and technology of their opponents, always learning from initial encounters and coming back the stronger.
- The later Republican period. Here, in 113 BC the Germanic Cimbri invaded Gaul from the far north. They carried all before them and were soon in conflict with Rome, the latter keen to protect its fertile Mediterranean province Transalpine Gaul. As in the dark days of the Second Punic War, the Romans once more struggled to contain a new foe (in that case Hannibal) and were defeated on the field of battle time and again. True grit once more showed through however, this time in the form of another great warrior consul, Gaius Marius. Realizing that the old manipular legions were no longer fit for purpose, he completely

reformed the Roman military. This featured the legions refounded as units of 6,000 men, with each legionary equipped in exactly the same way with *lorica hamata* chainmail hauberk, helmet, two *pilum* lead-weighted javelins and *gladius hispaniensis* sword. Further, of the 6,000 legionaries, 1,500 were also trained as craftsmen in the key skills needed to ensure the legion was completely autonomous and could operate without a lengthy supply train. Suddenly the legions were free to operate independently, or in ad hoc groupings as required. The speed that Marius utilized them soon wrong-footed the ponderous Cimbri migratory groupings, with the Germans massacred and Cimbrian Wars over. However, the Marian reforms of the legions had an unexpected outcome. This was because he also introduced regular pay for the legionaries for the first time, enabling rival Senators to raise their own legions that were ultra-loyal to them (Elliott, 2019, 24). Soon Rome was rocked by a series of vicious civil wars as rival *optimates* (pro-Senate and reactionary) and *populares* (radical) warlords strove for power, all driven by the prospect of controlling the huge amounts of wealth now entering Rome from the collapsing Hellenistic kingdoms in the east. Prime examples included Marius' great rival Lucius Cornelius Sulla, Gnaeus Pompey and Gaius Julius Caeser, and Mark Antony and Octavian (Goldsworthy, 2006, 425). As the first century BC neared its end it was the latter who, through luck and shrewd judgment, found himself the last man standing. Realizing stability was essential to ensure the survival of Rome, the Senate finally acknowledged him as *imperator* in 27 BC, and the Roman Republic came to an end. It is from that moment he took the name Augustus and became the first Roman emperor, finally bringing peace to the Roman world with his *Pax Romana*.

The Roman Principate
As detailed, the first phase of the Roman Empire is styled the Principate, the name derived from Augustus' title *princeps*, he using it to reference himself as the 'first among equals'. This phase, when Roman military power was at its strongest, lasted from 27 BC to AD 284. It featured eight distinct dynasties and periods, within which sat a number a major military campaigns. These included:

- The Julio-Claudian Dynasty, lasting from the accession of Augustus in 27 BC to the death of Nero in AD 68. This period included the beginnings of the empire, with Augustus securing his rule through a major restructuring of the military. This included reducing the number of legions he'd inherited from 60 to 30, these now comprising 5,500 men though still retaining the legionary specialist craftsmen of their Marian predecessors. He also reformed the naval power of Rome into regional fleets, with 10 eventually created. In terms of conflict, the Julio-Claudian period included Augustus' Cantabrian Wars in northern Spain, the loss of Varus' three legions in the Teutoburg Forest in AD 9, the Numidian revolt of Tacfarinas, and the initial campaigns of conquest in Britain from the Claudian invasion of AD 43 onwards.
- The 'Year of the Four Emperors' in AD 69, with Vespasian the ultimate victor.
- The Flavian Dynasty, from Vespasian's accession to the death of his younger son Domitian in AD 96. This included the defeat of the Batavian Revolt under Gaius Julius Civilis in AD 70, the later campaigns of conquest in Britain including the Governor Gnaeus Julius Agricola's campaigns in the far north, and the First 'Great' Jewish Revolt that lasted from AD 66 to AD 73.
- The Nervo-Trajanic Dynasty, from the accession of Nerva in AD 96 to the death of Hadrian in AD 138. This included Trajan's conquest of Dacia in two campaigns from AD 101 to AD 102 and AD 105 to AD 106, his Parthian campaign from AD 114 to AD 117, and the associated Second (Kitos War) Jewish Revolt from AD 115 to AD 117. The dynasty also featured the Third 'bar Kokhbar' Jewish Revolt from AD 132 to AD 135.
- The Antonine Dynasty, from the accession of Antoninus Pius in AD 138 through to the assassination of Commodus on New Year's Eve AD 192/193. The lengthy 23-year reign of Antoninus Pius was one of relative peace, with the empire at its most stable. However, the accession of the *diarchy* of Marcus Aurelius and Lucius Verus in AD 161 marked the beginning of a long period of trouble across Rome's far-flung frontiers. Most notable were the Roman-Parthian War from AD 161 to AD 166, and the lengthy Marcomannic Wars along the Danube that began in AD 166 and lasted well into the reign of Commodus in the AD 180s. The level of jeopardy faced by Rome in the latter series of

interlinked conflicts cannot be overestimated, with Heather describing 'the fires of war blazing all along Rome's European frontiers…' (2009, 94). Indeed, at one stage 'barbarian' incursions penetrated deep into north-eastern Italy, the first time the Roman homelands had been directly threatened since the Cimbrian Wars. Meanwhile, campaigning also occurred throughout this dynastic period in Britain, including the short-lived advance of imperial control up to the Antonine Wall on the Clyde-Forth line during reign of Antoninus Pius.

- The Year of the Five Emperors in AD 193, and the subsequent civil wars. The latter ranged from the accession of Publius Helvius Pertinax at the beginning of January that year through to the death of British governor and usurper Clodius Albinus in AD 197 at the Battle of Lugdunum (modern Lyon, Elliott, 2020b, 27).
- The Severan Dynasty, from the accession of Septimius Severus in AD 193 through to the assassination of Severus Alexander in AD 235. This included Severus' two campaigns in Parthia between AD 195 and AD 197, his campaigning in North Africa against the Garamantes Berber tribe, and his two attempts to conquer Scotland in AD 209 and AD 210 (Birley, 1999, 73). Later, Severus' elder son Caracalla also campaigned in Parthia (Sheppard, 2020, 60), while Severus Alexander fought unsuccessfully against the newly emerged Sassanid Persian Empire (which as detailed had replaced the Parthian Empire from AD 224) and the Germanic Alamanni and their Sarmatian allies.
- The 'Crisis of the Third Century', from the death of Severus Alexander to the accession of Diocletian in AD 284. This was a time when the empire was under great stress, racked with civil war and external conflict, pestilence in the form of the Plague of Cyprian, and economic depression. All ultimately led to change within and without its borders and the onset of the Dominate phase of empire. Much campaigning took place in this period, particularly against the Goths in Eastern Europe, and once more the Sassanid Persians. The low points were the advent of the breakaway Gallic Empire of Marcus Cassianius Latinius Postumus and his successors in the AD 260s and early 270s, and the capture and humiliation of the emperor Valerian by the Sassanid Persian king Shapur I at Edessa in AD 260 which for a time detached the eastern frontier away from the empire (Cornell and Matthews, 1982, 158).

The Roman Dominate

The 'Crisis of the Third Century' tested the integrity of the Roman Empire to its very limits, with Diocletian its ultimate saviour. Once in power he quickly realized that the imperial structure he'd inherited wasn't fit for purpose, and quickly set about a programme of widespread reforms.

In the first instance he instituted the *tetrarchic* system of political control that divided power across his vast empire between first two and then four (two senior and styled *augustus*, and two junior and styled *caesar*) brother-emperors. This final system with four emperors was officially instituted on 1 March AD 293, after eight years of dual rule.

Next, he completely reordered the provincial structure of the Principate in order to secure much firmer control of the tax base of the empire. He now created a new system of *diocese*, much larger units of economic control, to replace the older provinces. Each *diocese* was then broken down into a number of new, much smaller provinces.

Thirdly, by adding extra layers of public administration to support the above, he increased the coercive power of the Roman state. This allowed a fully systematized taxation regime to be introduced on all economic production called the *annona militaris*. In so doing he also issued a new, more stable currency that played a key role in curbing the rampant inflation that was a key factor in the economic woes of the 'Crisis of the Third Century'.

Finally, he decreased the political power of the military, and later carried out the first structural reforms of the military establishment for over a century. These were to see the armies of the later empire very different to those of the Principate.

There were a number of principal dynasties, time periods and large-scale military campaigns in the Dominate phase of empire. The key ones were:

- Diocletian's *tetrarchy*, from his accession in AD 284 until Constantine I secured control of the entire empire in AD 324. Military activity at this time included campaigns against the Germans and Goths on the Rhine and Danube frontiers, the usurpation of Carausius and Allectus, and the attempts by Maximian and Constantius Chlorus to defeat their North Sea Empire. The Romans also successfully campaigned against the Sassanid Persians.

- The Constantinian Dynasty from AD 324 through to the death of Jovian in AD 364. This dynastic period initially featured much civil war, with Constantine I seeking over time to control the entire empire following *legio* VI *Victrix* proclaiming him emperor in York in AD 306. There was also continuing trouble with the Germans and Goths along the Rhine and Danube, with Julian the Apostate's Alamannic War in Gaul in the AD 350s one of the better-known campaigns, and once more conflict in the east with Sassanid Persia.
- The Valentinian Dynasty from the accession of Valentinian I in AD 364 through to the death of the usurper Eugenius in AD 394. This period included the disastrous Gothic Wars of the eastern emperor Valens that culminated in the shattering defeat of the eastern field army at the Battle of Adrianople in AD 378. Here the emperor himself lost his life, and such were the Roman losses that the empire – both east and west – struggled to recover militarily afterwards.
- The Theodosian Dynasty, from the accession of Theodosius I in AD 392 to the death of Valentinian III in AD 455. Theodosius I was the last emperor to rule both the eastern and western halves of the Roman Empire at the same time. This dynastic period was dominated in the west by the widespread migration of Germans and Goths into the western empire, under pressure from the Hunnic expansion from the Asian steppe. It was bookended by two dramatic sackings of Rome, the first by Alaric I's Visigoths in AD 410 and the second by the Vandals under Gaiseric in AD 455. However, it was Hunnic predations in both the western and eastern empire that were to prove most problematic to its survival in the first half of the fifth century AD, with a military highpoint the defeat of Attila the Hun by the *magister militum* Flavius Aetius at the Battle of the Catalaunian Plains in AD 451.
- The Fall of the West, from the accession of Petronius Maximus in AD 455 to the abdication of Romulus Augustulus as the last western emperor in AD 476 on the orders of Odoacor, a senior officer in the Roman army. The latter, leading a revolt of *foederates* and regular units, had shortly beforehand been proclaimed *rex Italiae* 'king of Italy'. One of his first acts once in power was to send the regalia of western imperial authority to the eastern emperor Zeno, this officially marking the ending of the western empire. However, in the east it was to continue in one form or another until AD 1453 when the Ottoman Turks under the Sultan Mehmed II finally sacked Constantinople, destroying the last vestiges of the Byzantine Empire.

Specialist Roman Troops

The use of specialist troop types in a given army was not uncommon in the ancient world. For example, the early Chinese strategist Jiang Ziya detailed in his late second millennium BC treatise *Six Secret Teachings* the importance of recruiting warriors with specific skill sets into specialist units to perform key battlefield tasks.

Meanwhile, some argue the Skythian *hippotoxotai* who served in classical Athenian armies, and in the city itself as gendarmes, were also specialists. Mihajlov (2021, 12) details them defending the landing of Athenian hoplites on the island of Melos in 416 BC during the Peloponnesian War, with Thucydides saying the unit was 1,200 strong (*History of the Peloponnesian War*, 2.13). Alexander the Great also recognized the value of specialist troop types, for example the mountaineers he deployed when capturing the Sogdian Rock fortress north of Bactria in 327 BC (Johnson, 2021, 36). Later, the Carthaginian general and statesman Hamilcar Barca was well-known for deploying specialist troops, for example when commanding Carthaginian land forces in Sicily from 247 BC to 241 BC at the end of the First Punic War. He particularly favoured line-of-battle troops with naval experience to support amphibious operations. It is about Roman military specialists, however, that we know the most, given the comparative wealth of data available in primary sources and the archaeological record. I detail them here.

Pioneer and Engineering Specialists
The Marian legions of the later Republic, and Augustan legions of the Principate, all featured specialist pioneers who operated in the same manner as a modern combat engineer (Cowan, 2003a, 44). For example, they often deployed forward when the legion was on the march to select and prepare its marching campsite for the evening. These temporary fortifications were built every night when a Roman force was campaigning in enemy territory, featuring ditch, bank and palisade, with an interior replicating that of a permanent Roman fortification. I have also recently argued that similar marine pioneers from the regional fleets of the Principate built fortified assault harbours to speed the advance of legionary spearheads following coastal routes during Roman campaigns of conquest, for example that of Vespasian in the south-west of Britain with *legio* II *Augusta* in the later AD 40s (Elliott, 2016, 119).

Marian and Augustan legions also included a significant portion of their legionaries trained as specialist craftsmen. Here, the Antonine Prateorian Prefect Publius Terrutenius Paternus (in an extract included in the later *Digest of Justinian*, 50.6.7) usefully details many such specialists in his list of legionary *immunes* (soldiers exempted from general duties because of their specialist skills). These included ditch diggers, farriers, pilots, master builders, shipwrights, ballista makers, glaziers, arrow makers, bow makers, shield makers, smiths, coppersmiths, helmet makers, wagon makers, roof-tile makers, water engineers, sword cutlers, trumpet makers, horn makers, plumbers, blacksmiths, masons, woodcutters, lime burners, charcoal burners, butchers, leather workers and cobblers, huntsmen, sacrificial-animal keepers, grooms and tanners.

This range of specialist skills, and the scale of their output or contribution, would have been greatest in the legionary and vexillation fortresses and forts, for example being very visible at the fort at Vindolanda in northern Britain. There, references in the famous tablets speak of supplies of iron and lead, of smithing in general, of *scutarrii* (shield makers), and with archaeological data from spreads of tap slag, charcoal, ash and broken crucibles providing further clear evidence of extensive, self-contained metal-working and other related skills. These military workshops produced much of the weaponry and tools for their respective formations, over and above the large state-run *fabricae* that provided the legions with most of their equipment. The tablets also reference *sutores* (leather workers and cobblers), always in demand if only to maintain the tentage needed to keep the army in the field when on campaign. Here, some seventy goatskins were required for each tent, forty-eight of which were needed by even the smallest auxiliary unit.

Meanwhile, in addition to the specialists listed by Paternus, legionaries with construction skills were also much in demand given it was to the military the Roman state turned whenever a major engineering project began. Specific types included *agrimensores* land surveyors, *libratores* land levellers and *mensores* quantity measurers (Garrison, 1998, 75). In the case of the military building aqueducts, one can also add another specific type, the *aqualegus* aqueduct inspector.

Administrative Specialists

Roman military formations also included a range of specialist clerical staff drawn from the ranks, responsible for roles including the keeping of grain store records and also managing the financial accounts of the troops (Southern, 2007, 103). Details of such *immunes librarii* can be found from across the Empire, for example Septimius Licinius of *legio* II *Parthica* who set up a commemoration to a daughter in Albano, Italy, and Marcus Ulpius Firminus who similarly set up an inscription in Torda (Roman *Potaissa*) in Romania, then part of the province of Dacia.

The administration function performed by specialist clerical personnel in the legions also extended to the regional government of a given Roman province, certainly during the Principate phase of empire. Here, power was devolved from the emperor in the provinces through their governors and procurators in two separate chains of command, this system designed to prevent one or the other accruing too much power and challenging imperial authority. The former was the military and legal representative, the latter the financial secretary tasked with making the province pay.

To exercise their authority in the province, each governor headed an executive body called the *officium consularis*. In most provinces this included an *iuridicus* legal expert, *legate* senior commanders from any legions based there, Senatorial-level military tribunes from any auxiliary units, and junior officers. Meanwhile the procurator, always an equestrian so the level below Senatorial class, had a personal staff of equestrian and freedmen administrators called *procutatores* who were known collectively as the *caesariani* (Birley, 2005, 300). These personnel were registrars, finance officers and superintendents.

One might note here how small the executive teams of the governor and procurator were, in total no more than sixty staff in a normal province. To give context, in Roman Britain this amounted to only 0.0017 per cent of the estimated population of 3.5 million, compared to around 25 per cent in public employ today. Clearly this was an insufficient number of officials to run the province, and therefore both teams were bolstered by the appointment of military personnel assigned from the provincial military presence to assist with official duties. Those appointed to the *officium consularis* were known as *beneficiarii consularis*, and those to the procurator's staff *beneficiarii procuratoris*. A good example of an actual individual fulfilling one of these roles can be found in today's Museum of London, where the funerary monument of centurion Vivius Marcianus from *legio* II *Augusta* is displayed. Seconded from his legion's fortress at Caerleon in south-eastern Wales, he served as a *beneficiarii* based at the Cripplegate vexillation fort in London in the early third century AD.

Combat Specialists
Roman combat formations in both the Republic and empire also featured a wide variety of combat specialists whose skills were based on their place of origin or operation, or when a specific expertise was required to counter a new threat.

In the case of the latter, one of the most outlandish examples dates to the mid-Republican period and shows Roman military ingenuity at its most extreme. This was the invention of the anti-elephant wagon crewed by specially trained legionaries. These were invented to counter the elephants used by the Hellenistic king Pyrrhus of Epirus when he invaded Italy in 280 BC. There he fought three great battles against Rome, winning the first two narrowly but with heavy losses (hence the modern phrase Pyrrhic victory) and losing the third, again narrowly. In the first, at Heraclea in 280 BC, the Romans first encountered war elephants, the beasts playing a key role in Pyrrhus' costly victory. The following year at Asculum he again deployed his elephants in his line of battle, but this time the Romans were ready, trundling forward their newly designed ox-drawn anti-elephant wagons. These were equipped with long spikes to wound the elephants and pots of flaming oil on long poles to scare them, with screening light troops who hurled javelins and darts at the elephants to drive them away. Sadly for the Romans the effort came to naught as a final charge by Pyrrhus' elephants won the day, though again at great cost. The Romans would have to wait until the Battle of Beneventum in 275 BC to finally gain victory over the Epirots, there being no evidence the anti-elephant wagons were used here or indeed ever again.

Meanwhile, one of the best-known specialist units in the Principate Roman military were Batavian auxiliaries renowned for their skill in riparian operations along river systems and down coastlines. Recruited from their homelands in the Rhine Delta, these auxilia (both mounted and foot) are often referenced by primary sources carrying amphibious operations. For example, Batavian auxiliary cavalry are detailed in Germanicus' AD 16 campaign when forcing a crossing of the River Ems while fighting the Germanic Cherusci (Fields, 2020, 75). Here, Tacitus provides a vivid account of their skills when operating in such conditions, saying (*The Histories*, 4.12.3): 'These men were capable of swimming the Rhine while keeping hold of their arms, and maintaining perfect formation.'

However, it is Batavian foot auxiliaries who are best-known for their amphibious activities along river systems. This is in the context of the Aulus Plautius-led Claudian invasion of Britain in AD 43. Here, Cassius Dio details a river-crossing battle in the early stages of the initial conquest, this waterway often identified as the River Medway, with the actual battle site at Aylesford (Elliott, 2021b, 79). This proved a tough engagement for the Romans who were faced with the native British army arrayed on the western bank of the river. After the failure of the initial assault on the first day, Plautius' legionaries had to retreat to their marching camps on the eastern river bank where they were then harassed by British light troops. However, the experienced *legate* then used a clever stratagem to break the stalemate. Dio details this night-time operation in full, saying (*Roman History*, 60.20):

> [H]e sent across a detachment of Germans foot troops, who were accustomed to swim easily in full armour across the most turbulent streams. These fell unexpectedly upon the enemy, but instead of shooting at any of the men they confined themselves to wounding the horses that drew the chariots of the nobles; and in the confusion that followed not even the enemy's mounted warriors could save themselves.

One should note here the use of the term German rather than Batavian, though most interpret the former as the latter given their evident maritime prowess, and I agree.

Plautius' innovation proved a masterstroke, with the Romans able to force the river crossing the following day given the disorder among the British after their chariots and cavalry had been removed from the line of battle. A swift victory followed.

Then, later in the campaign after the Britons had fled north of the River Thames after defeat there in a second river-crossing battle, they were again pursued by Batavians, this time through marshes where they'd sought refuge (Zerdajtke, 2021, 27).

We have one last glimpse in the historical record of Batavians using their nautical skills. These are the auxiliaries who swam across the River Po near Placentia in Italy during the civil wars of AD 69 (Southern, 2013, 68). Here, fighting for the imperial candidate Vitellius, they succeeded in forcing the river by seizing islands ahead of a force of gladiators sent earlier by his rival Otho (Tacitus, *The Histories*, 2.35.1).

Meanwhile, as the Principate phase of empire progressed a variety of new types of *equites* auxiliary mounted troops appeared in the ranks of the auxilia. In the east these included specialist *equites dromedarii*, camel-mounted troops who were particularly suited to patrolling the arid desert *limes* there.

Such troopers initially appeared in the province of Arabia Petraea to the south of modern Syria, this largely a desert inhabited by nomadic and transhumant Arab peoples. For commerce this region relied on desert caravans operating through trading centres such as Petra, a town annexed by Trajan during his eastern campaigns, an event which initiated the creation of the province. One legion was based here, *legio* III *Cyrenaica* at Bosra (Roman *Bostra*), which was also the provincial capital. From there the legionaries and their supporting auxilia (including the *equites dromedarii*) had the unforgiving task of manning the southern *limes Arabicus*. Defence-in-depth is evident here, with the Romans frequently making use of their Ghassanid Arab allies to repel the Lakhmid Arabs who were supporters of the Parthians and later the Sassanid Persians.

Camel riding *equites dromedarii* were also found in Aegyptus, one of the powerhouse provinces of the empire, established in 30 BC after the then Octavian and his general Marcus Agrippa defeated Mark Antony and Cleopatra. Given its economic might, the province was always a place of difference within the empire, this based on the abundantly fertile Nile Valley that provided much of the grain supply to Rome and elsewhere across the Mediterranean. Aegyptus was also unique among Roman provinces in being considered the Emperor's own imperial domain where he was styled the successor to the preceding system of Pharaonic rule. Here the governor was a titled *praefectus augustalis*.

The legionary and auxilia presence in Aegyptus was deployed to counter the frequent native insurgencies in the province and also fought the nomadic Blemmye and Nobatae who lived in the desert between the Nile and Red Sea. Both of the latter, while not sophisticated opponents in terms of tactics and technology, often raided Roman Egypt in such numbers that they presented a real danger. The Romans countered this threat with a series of fortifications and watchtowers to protect the rich agricultural land in the Nile Valley. Most Blemmye and Nobatae warriors were unarmoured bowmen, often mounted on mules and donkeys, though they occasionally used elephants trained for war. Here the *equites dromedarii* came into their own, patrolling the Egyptian *limes* and desert interior. They are usually depicted in contemporary illustrations wearing *paenula* cloaks with the hood over the head to provide the trooper with shade from the intense sun, with local garments worn by the natives of the region also depicted. Such clothing, in association with auxiliary burials, has been found during archaeological investigations at Mons Claudianus and Didymoi, both in Egypt.

Some Roman combat specialists were also differentially armed to perform specific roles in the line of battle. For example the Romano-Gallic noble Julius Sacrovir, who rebelled against the imperial centre in AD 21, equipped some of his troops as very heavily armoured *crupellarii* gladiators to counter superior numbers of legionaries (Cowan, 2021, 11), while the emperor Aurelian made good use of Judaean warriors wielding two-handed clubs when fighting Queen Zenobia's Palmyran cataphract cavalry at the Battle of Emesa in AD 272. However, it is in the reign of Caracalla (AD 211–AD 217) that we see the emergence of a brand new type of specialist legionary. This was the *lanciarii* light trooper armed with a quiver of javelins and wearing a panoply of light armour. Such troops, who operated like the *velites* in the Polybian legions, skirmished forward to deter mounted bowmen and other lightly armed missile troops. They are first attested in gravestone epigraphy serving in the ranks of *legio* II *Parthica* in the context of Caracalla and Macrinus' AD 215–AD 218 Parthian War.

The late Roman period also saw a return to more glamorous specialist troops akin to those of the earlier Republic. For example, in his *Epitome of Military Science* Vegetius describes Roman crossbowmen called *arcubalistarii* who deployed alongside other skirmishing light troops (2.15). It is unclear if these were equipped with true crossbows, or a lighter man-portable development of the torsion-powered bolt shooters long used by the legions. However, elsewhere troops equipped with the latter are referred to as *manuballistarii*, perhaps indicating *arcuballistas* were indeed equipped with true crossbows. The only graphic evidence we have for such weapons comes from sculptural reliefs in Gaul where they are shown on hunting scenes, though sadly these do not show the release mechanism used on the weapon.

Meanwhile, the anonymous late Roman *De Rebus Bellicis* treatise on war highlights a number of specialist troop types and technologies it recommends should be adopted by the Roman military, which by this stage found itself under severe pressure along the Rhine and Danube, and in the east (12.14). The most outrageous was a stripped-down scythed chariot with only axle and scythed-wheels pulled by two cataphract fully-armoured lancers. However, there is no evidence this problematic design ever made it into production, let alone was used on the battlefield.

Elite Roman Troops

As with specialist troop types, elite warriors were also a common feature of armies in the ancient world. Think of the palace guard chariots of the New Kingdom Egyptian pharaohs often depicted on tomb artwork, Spartan *hippeis* hoplites, the Immortals of the Achaemenid Persian kings, and Alexander the Great's Companion shock cavalry. However, once more it is with the Romans where we have far more detail about their own elite troops. Most often this is in the context of guard troops, and here I begin with the Praetorians, arguably the ancient world's most famous such unit.

The Praetorian Guard

The use of elite Roman guard units had its origins in the Roman Republic. For example, at the time of the Punic Wars many guardsmen were recruited from Rome's Italian allies, Latin and otherwise. These were called *extraordinarii* who, as McNabb details, were (2010, 40) 'selected from the best allied troops, one third of the cavalry and one fifth of the infantry, who camped near the consul's tent and were at his immediate disposal.'

Later, various commanders began to assign crack troops to be their personal bodyguards, including Marius, Sulla and Mark Antony. Caesar himself used his own favourite legion, *legio X Equestris*, as his personal guard. However, the term Praetorian in the later Republic specifically related to the small escorts provided for high-ranking officials including leading senators, governors, proconsuls and procurators.

It was the first emperor Augustus who actually created the select force he styled the Praetorian Guard for his own personal protection. This comprised nine cohorts of 500 men, this later increasing to 1,000. He also added a small number of *equitatae* (Praetorian cavalry), these later replaced by the *equites singulares Augusti* imperial guard cavalry in the reign of Trajan. Later, his successor Tiberius (AD 14–AD 37) built the guard's *Castra Praetoria* fortified barracks to the immediate north east of the Servian Walls in Rome (Tacitus, *The Annals*, 4.1).

Next, Claudius increased the number of foot-guard cohorts to twelve, with Vitellius then increasing this again to sixteen during the 'Year of the Four Emperors' in AD 69 after disbanding the original nine. However, the ultimate victor in that struggle, Vespasian, decreased this to nine again.

Praetorian Guard cohorts rotated duty in the imperial palace on the Palatine Hill, with three on guard at any one time. As with the legions, the Praetorian Guard cohorts also included specialist craftsmen who were able to perform a wide variety of tasks when on campaign. A good example can be found on the tombstone of guardsman Caius Caristicus Redemtus in Brescel (Roman *Brixellus*) in Cisalpine Gaul who is described as a *plumba(rius) ordina(rius)*, this translating as a centurion-rank lead worker.

Praetorian Guards were well rewarded for their loyalty to the emperor. De la Bédoyère (2017, 32) records that Augustus ensured the Senate passed a law allowing him to pay them at least twice a legionary's salary. This was increased again by Domitian (AD 81–AD 96), and later by Septimius Severus. They also had better terms of service, only sixteen years compared to the legionaries' twenty-five. On retirement they were paid a huge gratuity of 20,000 *sestertii*, though given the many benefits of being a guardsman many re-enlisted. These were known as *evocatii Augusti*.

Early guardsmen, particularly in the reigns of Augustus and Tiberius, were recruited from existing legions and were experienced warriors, though as the Principate progressed this changed and they were increasingly recruited straight into the Guard. The Praetorians only left

Rome when on campaign with the emperor, which was more common at the beginning and end of the Principate.

Praetorian Guards were the only soldiers allowed in the *pomerium*, the sacred centre of ancient Rome, while bearing arms. This put them in a powerful position, particularly at times of imperial succession when they often played the decisive role if the throne was contested. However, they frequently overplayed their hand, for example when assassinating Pertinax who had succeeded Commodus in AD 193 at the beginning of the 'Year of the Five Emperors' (Elliott, 2020c, 155). Here they paid a high price, with the year's ultimate victor Septimius Severus cashiering the entire guard and banishing them from Rome. He then refounded the Praetorians at twice their original strength with his own Danubian veterans.

The Praetorian Guard was commanded by two Praetorian prefects, the first office holders being Quintus Ostorius Scapula and Publius Salvius Aper from 2 BC. From the reign of Vespasian these prefects were always equestrians, the appointment a serious career advancement. Many chose to monumentalise their success through public building works. A fine example can be seen today in Ostia Antica, the port of ancient Rome. Here the *forum* bath complex was built at the expense of the prefect Marcus Gavius Maximus.

When on campaign with the emperor, foot guardsmen were equipped in the same way as the better armed legionaries of the day. For the majority of the Principate this would have included two *pila*, a *gladius*, a *pugio* dagger and *scutum* shield (often featuring an image of winged victory, scorpions and crescents), and *lorica segmentata* banded iron armour (though *lorica squamata* scale-mail had begun to feature on images of guardsmen in contemporary sculpture). One point of the difference when compared to standard legionaries was the helmet, with Praetorians wearing particularly fine examples. These included exquisitely detailed Imperial Gallic types, as seen worn by a number of guardsmen on Trajan's Column, and also designs referencing the classical past. D'Amato and Sumner (2009, 206) say that Greek Attic helmets were a common type worn in that regard. The base uniform colour was red, with large white helmet plumes (red in the case of centurions and officers). When in Rome on escort duty, smaller oval shields and *lancea* light spears were carried, with the suit of armour replaced by a fine quality light toga.

The Praetorian Guard was always a potential source of instability in the imperial capital and was finally abolished by Constantine I in 312 after his defeat of his rival Maxentius (306–12) at the Battle of the Milvian Bridge. The victor then declared a *damnatio memoriae* against them, officially removing the Praetorians from imperial history, with the *Castra Praetoria* publicly dismantled. The *equites singulares Augusti* were also disbanded at the same time.

Later Roman Guard Units
Even before Constantine I's reform of the Roman guard corps, earlier emperors had moved to diminish the Praetorian Guard's power. For example, Diocletian had founded two new elite legions, *legio* V *Iovia* and *legio* VI *Herculia*, to operate as his own personal guard. These later became the Iovani and Herculiani legions that fought with distinction with Julian at Strasbourg in AD 357.

However, as part of his widespread reforms of the Roman military, it was Constantine I who finally tackled the troublesome Praetorians by disbanding them entirely. He replaced them, and the *equites singulares Augusti*, with new units of mounted guardsmen that he called the *scholae palatinae*. The term *schola* had formerly been used to indicate members of the imperial retinue, especially when the emperor was on the move. It now gave its name to the new, highly mobile units of guardsmen who accompanied the emperor at all times.

Each *scholae palatinae* unit comprised a *vexillatio*, just as with other late Roman cavalry units, and shared exactly the same organizational structure. They were commanded by a *tribunus militum*. However, unlike the troublesome Praetorian Guard, initially the new overall mounted guard had no single independent commander, with the emperor himself holding the post instead. Later, they came under the command of the *magister officiorum*, a new Master of Officers post established towards the end of Constantine I's reign to control not only the imperial guard but also the empire's civilian administration (Fuhrmann, 2012, 245).

There were initially five *scholae palatinae* units under Constantine I, this increasing to ten on his death, with five in the western half of the empire and five in the east. Those in the west were styled *seniores* and those in the east *iuniores*. The number of guard units continued to increase as the Dominate progressed, and by the time the *Notitia Dignitatum* was compiled in the late fourth and early fifth century AD there were eight *scholae palatinae* units in the west and seven in the east. In all phases of their existence the *scholae palatinae* also provided the emperor's close bodyguard. These totalled forty men chosen for their extreme loyalty who were named *Candidati* after their bright white uniforms.

Members of the *scholae palatinae* received benefits similar to their Praetorian Guard predecessors, including improved pay and conditions. They were equipped as standard *equites* but, given they were the elite cavalry of the late Roman army, with the finest possible armour and weaponry. However, just as with the Praetorian Guard, over time the *scholae palatinae* developed a reputation for enjoying life in the imperial capitals too much, particularly in the east. There, the emperor Leo I (AD 457–AD 474) eventually replaced them with a new guard unit called the *excubitores* (derived from the Latin term for sentinel) who were formed into a single unit 300 strong. However, in the west the *scholae palatinae* actually outlived the empire itself, being retained by Odoacer after he deposed Romulus Augustulus.

Finally, in the very late Dominate Empire another elite troop type emerged. These were the *buccellarii* (meaning biscuit eater), a term used to describe the mercenaries who often formed the personal bodyguards of military leaders and members of the aristocracy in this late period. They proved highly successful, and by the early sixth century AD had become a formal component of early Byzantine armies where they were styled *boukellarioi*.

Closing Discussion

As will be clear from the above narrative regarding Roman specialist and elite troop types, none of those considered here are likely candidates to be special forces based on the criteria set out in Chapter 1.

Chapter 3

Intelligence Gathering in the Roman World

Roman leaders in both Republic and empire prided themselves on the martial skills of their legions and auxilia. Every victory was applauded, every defeat lamented. Yet few *legates*, consuls or emperors chose to publicize the work of those gathering and analyzing intelligence, these often their most trusted advisors. This reflects the way the Romans chose to portray themselves, both to internal and external audiences, as worthy warriors who would never stoop to use the underhand strategies and tactics of their opponents. This was of course a classic Roman conceit, given the historical record shows that time and again the Romans used their full range of covert intelligence gathering techniques when required.

In terms of the Romans gathering intelligence, two kinds are considered in this book. The first is the acquisition of military intelligence, this certainly the remit of the various Roman special force candidates covered later, and so specifically considered in those chapters. The second is state-level intelligence gathering, using what today we might term a secret service. That is the main subject of this chapter where, for example, I detail the activities of the *frumentarii*, *agentes in rebus* and *notarii* who at various stages fulfilled this vital role. However, to provide context I first begin with a brief review of how the Romans policed their world.

Policing in the Roman World

Policing society at all levels was just as important in the ancient world as it is today, with the wider population's faith in its legal system vital to maintaining societal equilibrium. The Roman world presents a good case in point, given the insight we have here based on the written record and archaeological data. Fuhrmann provides a useful overview, saying (2012, 5):

Leaders in the Roman Empire (and earlier) had various means to stem the disorders they faced: community self-regulation, a well-developed civil law if that failed, the anxious supervision of local elites as a further safeguard, and, when necessary, the real threat of large-scale repercussions.

Roman law developed over a 1,000 year period, from the 'Twelve Tables' of the early Republic through to the codified reforms of Justinian I in the early sixth century AD. However, Rome had no single, holistic police force with which to enforce this legal system. While the modern word 'police' did originate in the classical world, deriving from the ancient Greek word *polis* meaning city-state, the concept of a modern police force is specifically applicable to our world today where it is laden with modern expectations. Instead, in the Roman world the law was enforced through a variety of different ways and means of coercion.

At its most basic one had elected magistrates who could appoint bailiffs and constables to maintain law and order, *fugitivarii* to catch runaway slaves (always an endemic problem in both Republic and empire), and citizen jurists who would enforce the law in court. Under this system, key aspects of legal activity were enacted in the *basilica* law court of a given settlement, a key feature of the urban landscape in all Roman towns and cities.

Much higher up the scale of legal responsibility one then had provincial governors and (once the Republic had transitioned to empire) imperially appointed procurators. As detailed in Chapter 2, the former was the emperor's legal representative in a given province, while the latter had responsibility for any legal matters relating to finance. Crucially, the governor and procurator were able to deploy an additional layer of law enforcement over and above the locally appointed bailiffs and constables to uphold the law. These were the *Vigiles Urbani* watchmen, and the *Cohorts Urbani* gendarmerie. Above that, in the case of serious societal disorder or where specialist investigative or legal skills were required, the state could finally turn to the front-line military.

Here I now briefly consider the Roman legal system given it informs the various law enforcement activities discussed here, and also provides the legalistic framework for state-level intelligence gathering considered later in this chapter. I then specifically look at the roles of the *Vigiles*

Urbanae and *Cohorts Urbanae*, before finally in this section focusing on the policing activities of the mainstream military.

Roman Law

Roman law was founded on the concept of the Twelve Tables, this a legal doctrine physically inscribed on twelve bronze tablets. The laws were created by a board of ten officials elected to design the new law code who took office in 451 BC, not long after the creation of the Republic with the overthrow of Tarquin the Proud in 509 BC (Potter, 2009, 50). They delivered their findings a year later in 450 BC, with the institution of their new system marking a brand new approach to legal matters in Rome whereby legislation passed by the Senate was then formally written down, allowing all citizens (at least in theory) to be treated equally in legal matters. Though not fully codified, the Twelve Tables were a major step forward allowing Roman citizens the right of legal protection, this for the first time permitting wrongs to be redressed through the use of precisely-worded laws known to all. This innovative approach, which focused mainly on private law and relations between citizens, was then widely copied across the classical world as the power of Rome spread, first through the western and then eastern Mediterranean. Sadly, the original bronze tablets were destroyed when the Senones Gauls sacked Rome in 390 BC after the Battle of Allia.

Roman law based on the Twelve Tables evolved as the Republic progressed, for example with the Licinian-Sextian laws passed in 367 BC which addressed the economic plight of the non-Senatorial classes in society. These were specifically designed to prevent patricians dominating the election of magistrates. Significant development then continued into the Principate phase of empire. Here, the first 250 years of the Christian era are still known as the classical period of Roman law, when leading jurists made substantial contributions to the body of legal doctrine, particularly Salvius Julianus who around AD 130 drafted a standard form of magistrate's edict which was used from that time to determine if a legal action was allowable, and was then due a defence in court. Later, around AD 160 the jurist Gaius codified all materials detailed in Roman legal cases into three categories, namely *personae* (individuals), *res* (things) and *actiones* (the legal actions themselves), a move which went on to underpin all future developments in Roman law.

These are just a few of the many refinements of the Roman legal system that took place over a 1,000 year period of jurisprudence (this the theoretical study of law) which culminated with the *Codex Justinianus*. Also known as the *Corpus Juris Civilis* (Body of Civil Law), this was the definitive collection of Roman laws and legal interpretations from the earliest days, codified under the sponsorship of Justinian I from AD 529 through to AD 564. Though not a new legal code, and using as its starting point the Theodosian Law Code of AD 438 (compiled under Theodosius II and Valentinian III), this collated in two reference works every past law and opinion in Roman legal history, including all of the ordinances of every Roman emperor, at the same time weeding out anything obsolescent or contradictory. To this Justinian then added a basic outline of the law as it stood at the time, including a collection of his own laws.

The two volumes of Justinian I's law code, comprising four specific books called the *Codex Constitutionum*, *Digest* (earlier referenced, also known as the *Pandectae*), *Institutiones*, and *Novellae Constitutiones Post Codicem*, proved to be Justinian I's greatest legacy, far outliving his reconquest campaigns in the west. Indeed, as Heather details, it proved a brilliant choice for a flagship home affairs programme (2018, 99):

> Justinian I's regime…had successfully fulfilled part of the remit of a fully legitimate, divinely appointed Roman ruler by bringing rational order to part of the written law which, at least according to its own self-understandings, distinguished this unique, divinely supported imperial world from every other society on earth.

As such, in a changing world after the collapse of the Roman west, Justinian I's *Codex Justinianus* stood out as a beacon of civilized stability. Soon the legal pronouncements of the Germanic and Gothic kings in their new territories in the west were being based on law codes heavily influenced by Justinian. These then continued to evolve over time as regimes came and went, and though the influence of Justinian's law codes waned over the years, even today they still form the basis of many aspects of modern legal systems across Europe.

Vigiles Urbanae and *Cohortes Urbanae*

In the built environment, to enforce Roman law above the level of locally appointed bailiffs and constables, Roman governors and procurators could also call upon the two other institutions detailed above. The first were the *Vigiles Urbanae*, originally founded by Augustus as a new public fire-fighting force in Rome based on the fire brigade long established in Alexandria, Egypt. These were colloquially known as *Spartoli*, or 'little bucket men', after the fire-fighting water buckets they carried. To pay for the new force Augustus levied a 4 per cent tax on all slave sales in Rome, and given the ever-present threat of conflagration in the imperial capital they proved highly successful. Soon, similar forces began to appear in towns and cities across the empire, where in the east they were known by their Greek name *nykto-philates*.

Given they were one of the few state-controlled bodies of men available outside of the mainstream military, the use of the *Vigiles Urbanae* soon spread to general public order tasks, and by the end of the first century AD they were being utilized in Rome and elsewhere as night watchmen. In that regard, Cassius Dio says that in his day in the late second and early third centuries AD they routinely carried bells to alert the general populace to any immediate threat of criminality or disorder, in much the same way a twentieth-century policeman might use a whistle (*Roman History*, 54.4.4). Commanded by an equestrian level *Praefectus Vigilum* in each place of use, the *Spartoli* proved one of the Roman Empire's most lasting institutions.

Meanwhile, having created his Praetorian Guard, Augustus soon found that deploying them on anything other than close protection duty in Rome was proving onerous to a Roman population keen to move away from having a regular military presence in the city after the final phases of Republican civil war. He therefore created a third institution to sit between the guard and his *Vigiles Urbanae* (at that time still only a new fire-fighting force), these the *Cohortes Urbanae* urban cohorts who were the equivalent of a modern *gendarmerie* armed police force. They originally numbered three cohorts of 500 men in Rome, each with 6 centurions and commanded by a tribune. They also proved highly successful, to the extent that by the time Tiberius became emperor after Augustus' death in AD 14 they helped him secure an easy transition to the throne, contrary to the expectations of many Romans (Fuhrmann, 2014, 123). Suetonius tells us that Tiberius came to increasingly rely on his urban cohorts to maintain public order in Rome, saying (*The Twelve Caesars*, Tiberius, 37.1): 'above all he was concerned to keep the peace from street violence, banditry and lawless dissension…he took zealous precautions lest popular uprisings arise, and severely repressed them when they started.'

An additional cohort was added in the Flavian period.

The urban cohorts in Rome were commanded by a *Praefectus Urbi*, a very high-level posting indeed given it was open only to Senatorial level former consuls appointed by the emperor (Fuhrmann, 2012, 117). This gave them tremendous personal power as they outranked the two prefects commanding the Praetorian Guard, and also the *Vigiles Urbanae* prefect, who were all equestrians. Meanwhile, just as with the *Vigiles Urbanae*, urban cohorts soon began to appear in other key towns and cities across the empire, though the commanders there were usually equestrians.

While not strictly front-line troops in the manner of legionaries and auxilia, the *Cohortes Urbanae* were often called on in times of crisis to bolster imperial armies in the field. One of the best-known examples was their use by the British usurper Clodius Albinus when fighting Septimius Severus at the Battle of Lugdunum in AD 197, he deploying a unit from the regional capital Lyon in his doomed bid for the throne. Meanwhile, an urban cohort from Rome itself later joined Severus' expedition to Britain in AD 208 (Elliott, 2018a, 143). However, for the most part the *Cohortes Urbanae* remained an armed policing force, their use continuing through to the end of the empire in the west in AD 476, and even later in the east.

The Roman Military in a Policing Role
Having discussed the Roman military as administrators in Chapter 2, I now consider their role in helping police the empire. In the first instance, resources from the legions were often called on if locally appointed bailiffs or constables, or the *Vigiles Urbanae* or *Cohortes Urbanae*, failed to deal with a troublesome local issue. We have direct evidence of this with, for example, a document from Egypt dated AD 207 detailing a senior centurion called Aurelius Julius Marcellinus investigating a complex case where a woman called Aurelia Tisais claimed her father and brother had been murdered on a hunting trip. Those under investigation included senior individuals in the regional administration, so the provincial governor chose to use the military directly to avoid the risk of

local coercion. Another document, dated to AD 193, details a centurion called Ammonius Paternus being contacted by a man called Syros who alleged that local notables were abusing their regional tax collection responsibilities. Again, here the governor turned to the legions given the unhealthy degree of local interest.

Such cases give insight into the daily function of the military carrying out everyday policing roles, in these and other cases the centurions in question having the power to make arrests and then seek judgment through the legal system and local magistracy, at least where the governor was convinced no corruption was involved.

Such activity is most evident in the east where, for much of the Principate certainly, the major legionary formations were based in or near major urban centres, for example Antioch-on-the-Orontes and Alexandria. As an example, in the case of the latter, the single legion garrison of the province of Aegyptus (from the time of Trajan *legio* II *Traiana Fortis*) was based at the legionary fortress of *Nikopolis* close to the provincial capital, while the *Classis Alexandrina* regional fleet was based in the city itself. Goldsworthy (2003, 143) argues that, given their huge populations, such cities often experienced turbulent unrest, with the military presence there deployed to restore order with violent force when needed. This also occurred elsewhere in the empire, with Fuhrmann (2012, 125) detailing one such example when Tiberius sent a full legionary cohort and troops from a client kingdom to deal with an unspecified scandalous incident in Pollentia in northern Italy. The troops surrounded the town and imprisoned most of the adult population, who were then given life sentences in prison. Meanwhile, a cohort was similarly used by Nero to stamp out an insurrection in Puteoli in Campania in AD 58. The military was also the force deployed to deal with slave revolts, with Tiberius for example dispatching two cohorts of auxiliaries to deal with such an incident in southern Italy in AD 24.

The Roman Secret Service

State level intelligence gathering in the Roman world was the responsibility of a complex network of spies, informers and analysts that evolved over time, this only fully maturing during the later Principate phase of empire. By that time it had evolved into what today we would call a secret service akin to MI5 in modern Britain or the Federal Bureau of Investigation (FBI) in the US, though with some resources focused externally as well as internally.

The Roman secret service had four key areas of responsibility, these being:

- The direction and targeting of information to help achieve Roman ambitions, or damage those of opponents, whether internal or external.
- The collection of data useful to the Roman state, this particularly focused on identifying societal unrest.
- The analysis of the gathered data.
- The dissemination of the gathered and analyzed data to those best able to make use of it.

Surprisingly, during the Republican and early Principate periods there was no official Roman secret service, the state keen to focus instead on its martial prowess. This was rooted in Rome's early Republican history when the central apparatus needed to effectively run such an operation ran counter to the Greek and Republican Roman city state ideals of oligarchical (and sometimes democratic) government. Here, honesty and transparency were the most valued traits among the ruling classes, they disdaining what they perceived as the underhand methods of their opponents. Indeed, the only Greek state which championed any form of secret service was Sparta, the most militaristic, and that only in the context of the *krypteia* set up to counter slave revolts by the *helots* who made up a significant portion of Spartan society (Sinnigen, 1961, 65). Additionally, the Senate and later the early emperors were also fearful of the power such a centralized, information-focused organization might wield.

This lack of organized state-level intelligence gathering and dissemination is evident in some notable Republican Roman disasters when intelligence data was readily available to mitigate likely threats but not acted on in time, or simply ignored. Notable examples include Hannibal's invasion of Italy over the Alps in 218 BC at the beginning of the Second Punic War, the spectacular underestimation of the Germanic Cimbri through the early phases of the Cimbrian War from 113 BC, and the high profile assassination of Julius Caesar on 15 March 44 BC. In the latter case, the dictator had a list of key conspirators actually handed to him shortly before he was murdered, but simply failed to read it (Elliott, 2019, 144).

The latter is an extreme example of Roman hubris when it came to intelligence-based decision taking, which some of their more canny opponents understood and exploited. One of the best examples can be found in Mithradates VI Eupator, the Pontic king who fought three major wars with Rome between 89 BC and 63 BC. He personally took charge of his intelligence-gathering network, for example actually visiting the new Roman province of Asia (modern western Turkey) and Rome's ally Bithynia incognito to gather details of the region he intended to campaign in. Here the second century AD Roman historian Justin provides much detail, saying (*Epitome of the Philippic History of Pompeius Trogus*, 37.3.4):

> His thoughts now moving to Asia, he set off in secret from his kingdom with some friends and roamed all over that country, with none aware of his presence, familiarizing himself with the location of all its cities and the geography of the land. He then went to Bithynia where, as though he were already master of Asia, he surveyed all the areas that would favour his victory.

Naco del Hoyo (2013, 407) stresses a key aim of Mithradates here was to determine Roman military strength and dispositions in the region, adding that the king had a year earlier opened lines of communication with rebel Italian cities at the time of the Social War around 90 BC. One primary source goes further, the Greek first century BC historian Diodorus Siculus saying that the Pontic king actually hosted an Italian delegation in his capital city Sinope (*Library of History*, 8.5). Thus, by the time the First Mithradatic War began, Mithradates had a clear picture not only of his Asian campaigning theatre and the Roman dispositions there, but also of Rome's foreign policy intentions and of Roman support for the conflict back in Italy. The Pontic king's lines of communication with Italy continued to prove useful, such that twenty years later during the Third Mithradatic War he was still being kept regularly appraised of developments there, for example the progress of the Third Servile War following the slave revolt led by Spartacus.

Sinnigen argues that it was only during the savagery let loose in the Republican civil wars of the first century BC, when the *optimates* and *populares* turned on each other with truly violent intent, that an unofficial secret service began to emerge in Rome. As he explains (1961, 65):

> During that era, warring dynasts turned to trusted soldiers, sometimes chosen for their private military entourage, to ferret out information and, as officers of arrest and execution, to do the 'dirty work' that one might expect of a secret police.

A prime example of their work would be the sanguineous proscriptions of the leading *optimas* Sulla in 82 BC when appointed dictator. Here, his informants turned on the supporters of his great rival Marius with brutal vengeance (Fuhrmann, 2012, 96). After exhuming the seven-time consul's body and throwing it in the Tiber, they then publicly identified thousands of Sulla's *populares* opponents, listing them on parchment nailed to the *curia* Senate House door. Those so proscribed were then rounded up and killed, with Sulla offering a reward to the citizens who actually carried out the deed. Rome turned into a bloodbath (Elliott, 2019, 67).

This set a pattern for the various stages of civil war that followed, through to the eventual success of Augustus who, as last man standing among his political rivals, was declared *imperator* by the Senate in 27 BC. However, even he was loath to entrust state-level intelligence gathering to one organization, he continuing to use a network of informal spies and informers instead. By this time, such operatives were known as *delatores*. This referenced the act of *delatio*, the legal denunciation of one private citizen by another (Fuhrmann, 2012, 151). Augustus' decision not to create a centralized secret service was in keeping with his other decisions regarding the military establishment he inherited. Fearful of any coalescence of power that might counter his new imperial project, he diluted critical mass at every opportunity. A prime example was his abolition of the single Mediterranean-based Roman fleet with its hundreds of war galleys. Instead he replaced it with a series of regional fleets based around his new empire, these eventually numbering ten.

As the Principate empire transitioned through its early Julio-Claudian and Flavian phases, each new emperor continued Augustus' policy of informal intelligence gathering, though increasingly state-level assets were used where they could be trusted, particularly tribunes and centurions from the Praetorian Guard. These often operated in plain clothes to gather intelligence, and were also empowered to arrest those suspected of treason.

Emperors also used military assets when the assassination of high-level targets was required. The most extreme example in the early Principate was the AD 59 matricide of Agrippina the Younger, mother of Nero. The reasons behind this are not fully understood, though according to Tacitus Nero's affair with Poppaea Sabina was the trigger behind their dramatic falling out given the latter was already married to the leading Senator and future short-lived emperor Otho (Tacitus, *The Annals*, 14.1). In that context, the affair could therefore have put the imperial family at risk, especially as Agrippina was close to Nero's wife Claudia Octavia.

Nero's attempts to murder his mother were outlandish to say the least, with Suetonius saying he ordered Anicetus, admiral of the *Classis Missenensis* regional Tyrrhenian fleet, to arrange a shipwreck using a collapsing boat (*The Twelve Caesars*, Nero, 34.1). However, Agrippina, a good swimmer, survived and swam ashore. Her survival was to no avail though as she was later executed by Anicetus, who stabbed her to death in her villa assisted by a fleet centurion; they then reported her death as a suicide. Sadly for Anicetus this proved the 'high' point of his career as, after the murder of Agrippina, Nero forced him to confess to committing adultery with his wife Octavia, after which she was banished and later died a miserable death. Anicetus himself was banished to Sardinia where he lived out his days in comfortable exile before dying of old age.

Despite Nero's excesses, which eventually caused his downfall, Roman emperors continued to resist creating a formal secret service. However, this changed with the accession of the ill-favoured Domitian, last of the Flavian emperors, in AD 81. Increasingly unpopular in Rome, he carried out a number of reforms of the apparatus of imperial government, aiming to accrue more power. This included restructuring the *frumentum* supply section of the *praetorium* imperial general staff, whose name derived from an early Roman term for wheat distribution, and it is here that he chose to establish his new formal secret service. Its new members were recruited from the logistics specialists based in the *frumentum*, these often former soldiers of non-commissioned officer rank, where they were already known as *frumentarii*. This now became the name for Rome's first official secret agents. As Sinnigen (1961, 66) says, it therefore seems the first official Roman secret service 'was staffed by supply sergeants whose original functions had been the purchase for and distribution to the troops of grain.'

Frumentarii *and the Roman Secret Service*
While it might seem odd that Domitian chose the *frumentum* as home to his new secret service, it actually made perfect sense, with Sinnigen adding (1961, 66):

> Commentators believe that the members of the frumentum were already constantly on the move on logistical assignments at an early date, and that they were in constant touch not only with the army and bureaucracy, but with the provincial population as well.

Further, the logistics function of the *frumentum* had been made much easier by the time Domitian was emperor given the earlier reforms of the Roman transport network by Augustus. Thus the officials of the *frumentum*, already travelling on official business throughout the empire using imperial trunk roads and *mansio* official way stations, were ideally placed using their widespread military and commercial contacts to form the basis of the new Roman secret service. There is some confusion here about whether the terms *frumentum* and *frumentarii* continued in use in their original logistical context after this time given their new espionage association, but for clarity from this point I will only use them with regard to the latter.

Domitian also created a headquarters for his new secret service. This was located at the Castra Peregrina 'camp of strangers', an old Republican military barracks on the Caelian Hill, situated between the Temple of Claudius and Nero's Macellum Magnum market. This was a very fashionable district in Rome and home to many of its wealthiest families, and only a short walk from the Palatine Hill and *Forum Romanum*. It was thus ideally placed to help the *frumentarii* keep track of the activities of Rome's leading citizens. Domitian also created a new post to command his secret service, the *Princeps Peregrinorum* who reported to the *Praefectus Urbi*, head of the *Cohortes Urbanae*. Unsurprisingly, soon the *frumentarii* and urban cohorts were working closely together. Additionally, as the secret service matured, a *frumentarius* was also added to the staff of the key provincial governors across the empire.

A surprising amount is known about the *frumentarii* despite the fact they were a secret service, this largely from inscriptions on tombstones and commentary from contemporary historians. For example, for much of their existence they wore an official uniform when not operating covertly, this to ensure good behavior from all in their view. Additionally, funerary stele show that over time they were increasingly recruited direct from the ranks of the legions rather than as former soldiers in the employ of the state logistics service.

Interestingly, Roman emperors initially chose not to keep their activities completely secret, with some *frumentarii* overtly allocated to specific legions on a permanent basis. In that regard, if one were to draw a direct modern parallel, at this early stage in their existence it would be with military intelligence rather than a state-run secret service like MI5 or the FBI as they later became.

Clearly, transmitting information in a timely manner was vital for the successful operation of the new Roman secret service, especially given the distances involved. For example, sending a message from Rome to London could take up to thirty days, and that by the quickest route using imperial trunk roads, river systems and the sea. In the first instance, the emperor and his *frumentarii* could send intelligence through the *cursus publicus* imperial postal service. This was able to make use of the network of *mansiones* for rapid mount changes in the case of great urgency. However, if there was a traitor within the system, secret imperial communications could easily be compromised.

For example, Caracalla was almost warned of the fatal plot against him by his Praetorian prefect Macrinus (emperor from AD 217 to AD 218), his eventual successor. This came from Materianus, *Praefectus Urbi* commander of the urban cohorts in Rome. Crucially, this post gave Materianus responsibility for the *frumentum* when the emperor was away on campaign, a frequent occurrence with Caracalla. In that capacity his *frumentarii* got wind of the plot and soon a sealed message was on its way to the emperor using the *cursus publicus*. However, in a crucial error, the courier was not made aware of the key dispatch being carried among the emperor's normal post. Therefore, when Caracalla received the mail in Edessa on the eastern frontier in April AD 217, instead of reading it himself he gave the dispatches to Macrinus, including the warning from Materianus about the Praetorian prefect. The latter promptly disposed of the incriminating note, and now forewarned he was under suspicion of treason in Rome initiated his plot. He recruited a guard officer called Julius Martialis to kill the emperor whose brother had been executed by Caracalla. The assassin struck soon afterwards, stabbing the emperor to death while he was relieving himself against a tree while on the road to visit a temple at Carrhae (Scarre, 1995, 145). Such was the price of an intelligence failure for an unpopular emperor.

As time passed the *frumentarii* also began to take responsibility for political assassinations. For example one unnamed *frumentarius* centurion, with a reputation for killing Senators, was sent by the short-lived 'Year of the Five Emperors' candidate Didius Julianus to assassinate Septimius Severus as he approached Rome in AD 193 (Fuhrmann, 2012, 152). He failed, was executed, and Severus became emperor.

Another example was the murder of the Emperor Maximinus Thrax's former Praetorian prefect Vitalianus by the usurping Gordian I and Gordian II. Though based in North Africa, the latter were championed by the Senate in Rome who disliked Maximinus intensely. This gave them access to the *frumentum*, and soon *frumentarii* were on their way to remove the former prefect who was now the governor of the province of Mauretania Caesariensis. There he was still the sitting emperor's staunchest supporter and could challenge the two usurpers given they were based to the immediate east in Africa Proconsularis. To gain close audience the *frumentarii* disguised themselves as messengers from Maximinus Thrax himself. Once with the governor, while Vitalianus was examining the seals on their dispatches, they stabbed him to death with swords hidden beneath their cloaks.

The Late Roman Secret Service
As the Roman world transitioned the 'Crisis of the Third Century' the *frumentarii* were increasingly used by various emperors, often in post only a short time, to help secure faltering tax revenues. Never popular in the first place, they now became hate figures in wider society. As Sinnigen explains (1961, 69):

By the later third century AD at the latest, when the frumentarii were under increasing pressure from higher echelons to guarantee the flow of revenue…and to protect the security of an increasingly impoverished and apparently (certainly as it would have seemed at the time) disintegrating state, they were roundly hated by Rome's subjects.

Certainly, even before this time the *frumentarii* had developed a reputation for exceeding their authority. For example inscriptions from the wealthy province of Asia in western Turkey show farmers complaining bitterly at arbitrary arrests being made, and taxes exacted, by the local *frumentarii*. In fact, good behaviour towards the local population there was so unusual it was actually mentioned on the tombstone of a *centurio frumentarius* officer.

It therefore proved easy for Diocletian, as part of his widespread reforms of the imperial administration, to restructure the secret service into something more in step with his vision of running the empire. From this point we speak no longer of the *frumentarii*, but instead of two new branches of what became the late Roman secret service. These were the *schola agentes in rebus* ('corps of the general agents'), and the *schola notariorum* ('corps of imperial secretaries'). Here perhaps we can see the emergence of something more akin to a modern secret service, with the former tasked with direct action against the enemies of the state, and the latter the investigative branch.

The *agentes in rebus* and *notarii* were far more integrated into the Roman military establishment than their *frumentarii* forebears, with a formal recruitment structure that paralleled those of late Roman military units. This reflected Diocletian's desire to keep a much firmer grip on his levers of state.

The *agentes in rebus* featured five ranks of seniority, these the *equites*, *circitores*, *biarchi*, *centenarii* and *ducenarii*, all titles based on those used in late Roman cavalry *schola*. Their organization was further refined by Constantine I who, towards the end of his reign, placed them under the command of his new *magister officiorum* in the imperial court (Fuhrmann, 2012, 245). This led to the *agentes in rebus* also being called *magistriani*, though to avoid confusion here I will stick with their original name. Shortly after a new senior post was also created to manage the day-to-day activities of the *agentes in rebus*, the *princeps officii* who reported to the *magister officiorum*. This position was senior enough for some holders to be promoted to the post of *diocene vicarii* as the next step on the public-service career-path, the equivalent of the provincial governors of the Principate.

We have much insight into the activities of the *agentes in rebus* thanks to detail provided by contemporary writers. For example, during the reign of Constantius II the service was tasked with investigating Claudius Silvanus, a senior Roman general of Frankish descent. He initially supported Magnentius when he usurped against Constantius in AD 350, but defected to the emperor at the Battle of Mursa Major in AD 351. After that he proved a highly capable leader in imperial service and soon Constantius promoted him to the rank of *magister peditum per Gallias*. This in effect put him in charge of the whole of Roman Gaul. From there he then led successful campaigns across the Rhine against the Germanic Alamanni, further endearing him to the emperor. However, his success made him enemies in court where members of Constantius' *praetorium* advisory council persuaded the ever-suspicious emperor that Silvanus was planning a coup.

According to Ammianus Marcellinus (*The Later Roman Empire*, 15.5.15), as evidence the conspirators used a sponge to alter a letter sent by Silvanus to his friends in the Senate in Rome, with the altered document suggesting he was attempting to win their support for a bid for the throne. Then two other courtiers called Apodemius and Dynamius forged further letters aiming to cast even more doubt on Silvanus' loyalty. It was at this point the investigating *agentes in rebus* were called into action in Milan (Roman *Mediolanum*) where Constantius was based. They quickly found all of the correspondence in question to be forgeries, exonerating Silvanus. However, back in Gaul the Frank was unaware he'd been found innocent and, knowing the accusations against him could lead to his execution, actually did proclaim himself emperor on 11 August AD 355 in Cologne (Roman *Colonia Agrippina*). Sadly for him the desperate move proved a dramatic failure, with his usurpation lasting only a few weeks before he was hacked to death by Gallic soldiers recruited by agents working for Constantius (Langenfeld, 2021. 42.2). Given one of those sent to investigate him was the late Roman historian Ammianus Marcellinus we have much detail here, this recounted in full in Chapter 5 given he was a *protector domesticus*, such imperial guardsmen being considered as special force candidates in that chapter.

Meanwhile, a key role the *agentes in rebus* took on as the Dominate progressed was surveillance of the various new ministries of state created by Diocletian. Here, the imperial court would send intelligence officers to each department of state to spy on those running them, the aim to ensure their loyalty to the sitting emperor. In this role they proved particularly effective, with the late fourth century AD rhetorician Libanius saying they were the surest means of detecting corruption, especially at a senior level (*Oratio*, 18.80).

Though we have no detail about the numbers recruited to serve as *agentes in rebus* in the Western Empire, we do in the east. Here surviving legal documents show that in AD 430 Theodosius II tried to limit their numbers to 1,248, while later Leo I cut this to 1,174 in AD 460 (Kelly, 2004, 20). This shows two things in particular. First, a degree of distrust still existed between later emperors and their security apparatus given these attempts to limit their numbers, and so their power. However, it also shows the longevity of the *agentes in rebus* given here they are still in operation in the east as the empire in the west neared its end. Indeed, they survived in the east until at least the seventh century AD, with the last mention of the *agentes in rebus* that by the late eighth century AD Byzantine chronicler Theophanes the Confessor who details the *magistrianos* Paul being sent on an embassy in AD 678 (*The Chronicles of Theophanes*, 61.78).

Moving on to the *notarii*, as detailed this was the investigative branch of the late Roman secret service. Its members were recruited with specialist legal and literacy skills in mind, initially direct from the ranks of the palace guard given the close access this branch of the late Roman secret service had with the emperor. Later, its ranks were opened to gifted individuals from the wider civil population. These included Senators of the highest rank and lowly freedmen, with recruitment based on capability. Sinnigen paints a detailed picture of this later *schola notariorum*, saying (1959, 244):

> On the whole, the corps presents a composite picture of able and literate men recruited from many walks of life, some of whom have been recruited because of their potential capacities for dealing with difficult and delicate situations.

Admission to the ranks of the *notarii* was open not just to Roman citizens but also others from outside mainstream Roman society. For example, one senior fifth century AD agent was a native German.

Given the *notarii* performed the clerical duties of the secret service, this gave them great power, especially as a key task was that of imperial note-taker on the emperor's behalf. If your name appeared in one of their documents, you were in real trouble. One of the most infamous members of the *schola notariorum* was Paulus *Catena* (Paul the Chain), a leading inquisitor under Constantius II (AD 337–AD 361). He was dispatched to Britain in the wake of the failed revolt of Magnentius to bring the troublesome province back into the imperial fold, having already tracked down and executed the usurper's supporters in Gaul. Notorious across the empire for his cruelty, his nickname either referenced his ability to weave chains of intrigue around those he was interrogating, or a form of torture whereby the unfortunate victim was weighed down with increasing volumes of chains until they confessed. He specifically targeted the elites of late Roman Britain, to the extent that the *vicarius* Martinus attempted to assassinate him and, failing, then committed suicide rather than face trial. Paulus himself later met a fitting fate, being burned to death by Julian the Apostate after being tried for treason at the Chalcedon tribunal in AD 361.

Senior members of the *schola notariorum* could also cause trouble in other ways. For example, we know of at least three senior *notarii* who launched unsuccessful usurpations against sitting emperors in the late fourth and early fifth centuries AD. Another former *notarii* actually did become emperor, and a disastrous one at that, this Petronius Maximus who reigned for twelve weeks in AD 455. Here I briefly detail his life and career given it shows how having early access to the resources of the *schola notariorum* could seriously benefit the ambitious.

Maximus was born in AD 397 to a well-connected Senatorial family, he enjoying a remarkable early career on his *cursus honorum* aristocratic career path. This included holding key posts in the *schola notariorum* while still a teenager, where he was soon appointed a senior agent. Maximus then used his connections in the secret service to accrue a series of other key postings in the imperial administration, for example serving as the *comes sacrarum largitionum* in court between AD 416 and AD 419. This was a powerful position indeed given it gave him financial control of key sectors of the Roman economy, including the emperor's imperial estates, taxation of Senators, custom duties, the various large scale *metalla* mining industries across the empire, mills and textile factories, and mints (Scarre, 1995, 231).

While still maintaining his position within the *schola notariorum*, Maximus was then promoted to become the *Praefectus Urbi* urban prefect in Rome, giving him control of the municipal administration of the city. He later became the *praetorian prefect* at court, this now the title of the emperor's senior military and legal advisor rather than guard commander after the Praetorian Guard had been abolished, before becoming *Praefectus Urbi* again in AD 439. During this period he was also appointed consul. In the AD 440s he was then placed in charge of the praetorian prefecture of Italy, all the time still using his connections within the *schola notariorum* to his advantage. Though we have no specific detail, it seems likely that by this time Maximus was in full control of the *schola notariorum* given his unfettered career progress, whether officially or not.

Maximus was awarded a second consulship in AD 443, and then granted the official title *patrician*, the empire's senior honorific title. This set him on a collision course with Rome's most senior *magister militum*, the great Flavius Aetius who was later to defeat Attila the Hun at the Battle of the Catalaunian Plains in AD 451. To show his largesse and get one over on his rival for imperial attention, Maximus then built his own forum in Rome in AD 445 called the *Forum Petronii Maximi* on the wealthy Caelian Hill. However, after Aetius' defeat of the Huns he found himself increasingly sidelined, and decided to act. Ever the spymaster, he began a campaign to blacken the name of Aetius at court, targeting those with the emperor Valentinian III's ear. Once the seeds of discord had been sown Maximus persuaded the emperor's *primicerius sacri cubicili*, who was in charge of the imperial household, to become a fellow conspirator. This was the eunuch Heraclius, and together they convinced the emperor that Aetius was planning a coup. Even Maximus was surprised at his own successor when, without warning, on 21 September AD 454 Valentinian himself stabbed Aetius to death in a fit of rage during an audience, with Heraclius joining in (Goldsworthy, 2009, 333).

Sadly for Maximus there was no immediate reward for him. Valentinian had spent much of his reign under the control of others. First, his mother Gallia Placidia had long been his regent. Later, Aetius' enormous success as a military leader had overshadowed anything the emperor could achieve. Now free of his dominating *magister militum*, Valentinian was free to rule as he wished. Far from being the new power behind the throne, Maximus now found himself just another advisor. This did nothing to diminish his ambition, and soon the emperor himself became the new target for the ever-scheming *notarius*. Maximus convinced two palace guards called Optila and Thraus-tila, both former Aetian loyalists of Hunnic origin, to kill Valentinian. This they did on 16 March AD 455, also killing Heraclius in the process. The assassins then duly took the imperial diadem to Maximus, who the day after became emperor (Heather, 2005, 374). The spymaster had now risen to the very top of the imperial tree, though it wasn't to last, with his fall now dramatic and fatal.

In the first instance Maximus quickly married Valentinian's widow, Licinia Eudoxia. However, he now made a huge mistake, cancelling the marriage of Licinia's daughter Eudocia to Hunneric, son of the Vandal king Gaiseric. By this time the latter was in full control of Roman North Africa, and fabulously wealthy. While keen to integrate his migratory peoples into the pre-existing imperial administration in what was still the richest part of the Mediterranean world, Gaiseric was still a proud Germanic king. He took great offence at Maximus' seemingly arbitrary decision, and soon word reached Italy that Gaiseric was sailing with a vast fleet, his target Rome. This caused blinding panic there, with many inhabitants fleeing. It was at this point Maximus had a disastrous crisis of confidence. He chose to flee himself, hoping to reach Ravenna in northeastern Italy where he would be secure behind its extensive marshes and wetlands. However, he had barely left Rome on 31 May when his bodyguard abandoned him. Shortly after he was found by an angry mob, quickly set upon, and stoned to death. His body was then mutilated, and in a final humiliation his corpse thrown in the Tiber. The Vandals then duly sacked Rome, and far more severely than the Visigothic sacking of AD 410. In this instance, the Vandal king's sword really did prove mightier than the former *notarius*' pen.

Returning to the *schola notariorum*, this reported directly to the emperor, who appointed a *primicerius notariorum* to supervise its activities. This was a very senior position in the late Roman imperial hierarchy, which as indicated Maximus may have held. As an example of its importance, the holder of this post was responsible for compiling and updating the

Notitia Dignatatum list of public office holders, one of our key sources for the later Roman Empire today.

From the time of Julian in the AD 350s some members of the *notarii* were also tasked with passing unwritten imperial orders to *diocene vicarii*, provincial governors and military leaders, a shrewd way to avoid embarrassing audit trails. In one example, Valentinian I sent a leading *notarius* to order the *dux* along the Rhine frontier to begin building defences there, and just in time given the subsequent Germanic invasions were repelled. These specialist *notarii* were also called *referendarii*, their activities continuing in the west after the ending of the empire there in AD 476. As time progressed they became even more important in the post-Roman bureaucracy in Italy, and by the time of the later Ostrogothic kings of Italy had become the last surviving members of the *schola notariorum*. In the eastern empire such specialist *notarii* continued in use, their name changing over time to *a secretis*, or *asekretis* in Greek.

Closing Discussion

In this chapter I have detailed the Roman security personnel who carried out judicial and extra-judicial operations on behalf of the state outside the remit of normal policing. These included the plain-clothes tribunes and centurions of the Praetorian Guard in the Principate, the *frumentarii* in the same period, and later the *agentes in rebus* and *notarii* of the Dominate. However, while most of their actions were of the deniable type, and many were elite volunteers, the personnel so engaged were not uniquely trained for non-regular warfare, particularly as their main focus was internal affairs. Additionally, they were certainly not used to secure operational and strategic advantage in conflict, unless in a civil war context. Therefore, once again, here we have no candidates that we may consider special forces in a modern context.

Chapter 4

Speculatores and *Exploratores*

Having considered state-level intelligence gathering in Chapter 3, I now move on to examine how the Romans in both Republic and empire gathered military intelligence, at both a strategic and tactical level. This naturally leads to an analysis of how such intelligence was used in special operations, and the bespoke forces that carried them out. It is in this context we now get to examine in detail the first two credible candidate units we might consider special forces, the *speculatores* and *exploratores*.

The *speculatores* were initially the scouting and reconnaissance specialists in the late Republican and early Principate legions whose role over time expanded, first to cover troops engaged in covert operations at a tactical level, and then later various types of legionaries or military personnel tasked with an exceptional role (Austin and Rankov, 1995, 9). Meanwhile the *exploratores* initially worked alongside the *speculatores*, it being difficult to separate their activities early on. However, they evolved to become the strategic eyes and ears of the Roman military, offensively in support of major campaigns and, later, defensively across the empire's widespread frontiers as imperial expansion turned to consolidation. They specialised in long-range covert operations, somewhat akin to the British LRDG detailed in Chapter 1, operating deep in the enemy interior in support of advancing legionary spearheads when on campaign, or helping mitigate the intense migratory pressures later experienced by the empire along its extensive borders. Today we would call the role they performed deep reconnaissance/strike, and this is where we begin to see a true differentiator between the *exploratores* and the *speculatores*, the former operating at a more strategic level, and with the ability to engage in offensive operations more effectively. It is with the *exploratores* that we get some of our best insight into Roman special operations through the use of specific examples, for example the Marcomannic Wars of Marcus Aurelius and Lucius Verus in the later second century AD, and

Julian's campaigns against the Alamanni in the AD 350s (Elliott, 2020a, 225). However, I first begin the chapter with a brief review of military intelligence in the Roman world to provide context for what follows.

Note that some consider the roles of the *speculatores* and *exploratores* to be interchangeable throughout their existence and not just early in their use, or even to be the reverse of how I present them here. However, what you read here is my own interpretation based on a detailed examination of the hard data. Specifically, I have tried to set in place a structure to aid understanding of what is an often-confusing use of nomenclature by both contemporary and modern commentators.

Finally, also note that the activities of *speculatores* and *exploratores* in the later empire are considered in Chapter 6 when the use of such names becomes even more problematic, this at a time when other Roman special force candidates begin to appear.

Military Intelligence in the Roman World

In the ancient world direct contact between combatants was often closer, more frequent and more deadly than in the modern world given the obvious lack of sophisticated long-range surveillance and battlefield weapons of mass destruction. Therefore early notice of the proximity of an opponent and their intentions was vital, and often campaign and battle winning. In the Roman world this was provided by military intelligence resources of a variety of kinds, these all examined in this and subsequent chapters.

To help guide our understanding here, Austin and Rankov have usefully defined how military intelligence operated in the Roman world at both a strategic and tactical level. They say (1995, 7):

> We have attempted to define strategic intelligence as the analysis of everything that happens before the arrival at the battlefield, and this would include any long-term information that would influence the conduct of the whole campaign, the capacity of an enemy to wage war and his intention to do so. Tactical intelligence would take over at the point where the two sides are nearly in sight of each other and includes short-term material influencing the choice of a battlefield, the positions taken up on that battlefield and the conduct of the fighting itself.

This is a common-sense interpretation that I will use in this book, and which is also reflected in our key primary sources. For example Vegetius goes into great detail in his *Epitome of Military Science* about the kinds of information needed at a strategic and tactical level in any briefing given to a commander (3.6). He says that at the higher level a commander should be briefed on his opponent's strengths and weaknesses as a leader, about the nature of the opposing army and quality of its warriors, and about their levels of provisioning. Meanwhile, at the tactical level Vegetius adds that close attention needs to be paid to gathering intelligence regarding the battlefield itself, and particularly the approach to the site to avoid an ambush. He concludes that gathering and disseminating this military intelligence, at both a strategic and tactical level, should be a continuous process, with the commander in the field regularly updated (*Epitome of Military Science*, 3.9).

Other Roman commentators also promoted the importance of military intelligence, and at a time Roman leaders were still eschewing the overt use of a secret service to gather state-level intelligence. For example, in a negative context, Tacitus argues the 'Year of the Four Emperors' candidate Aulus Vitellius was a prime example of military ineptitude given he showed no knowledge of the need for military intelligence on campaign or in battle (*The Histories*, 3.56). Emperor for just eight months in AD 69, Vitellius was a man better known for his love of fine living who Wellesley calls a lethargic non-entity (1989, 9), while Austin and Rankov speak of his military incompetence (1995, 7). These were all traits born out in his epic failure as a military leader.

Earlier, Caesar showed understanding of the importance of military intelligence at both a strategic and tactical level, and to a standard recognizable in modern conflict. Military training manuals today use a five point system to show how information can be turned into intelligence, these being:

- Definition
- Collection
- Collation
- Evaluation and Interpretation
- Dissemination.

Examples of all can be found in Caesar's own detailed accounts of his Gallic conquest campaigns in the 50s BC. For example, with regard to evaluation and interpretation, this can be seen writ large in his 53 BC campaign against the rebellion of Ambiorix, leader of the Eburones Belgic tribe. This followed total Roman humiliation at the beginning of the year when the Eburones besieged a major Roman base in northern Gaul housing fifteen cohorts of legionaries led by the *legates* Lucius Aurunculeius Cotta and Quintus Titurius Sabinus. The force included the entire *legio* XIV. Here Ambiorix had offered the Romans safe passage south to join other nearby Roman units but Cotta and Sabinus argued over their response, the former saying their orders from Caesar were to remain where they were in their well-protected and provisioned camp. However, the latter argued they should accept the offer, and he prevailed. Early the following morning the camp was struck and the cohorts of legionaries left in good order. Sadly for the Romans it was a Gallic trap, the column being ambushed near modern Tongeren in Belgium. It was wiped out almost to a man, despite fighting valiantly. Satisfied with their good work, the Eburones returned to their towns and villages with any loot they could gather from the destroyed Roman cohorts (Elliott, 2019, 118).

Caesar, at the time in southern Gaul, sped north with characteristic decisiveness with as many of his troops as he could muster, arriving just in time to prevent the loss of another legion. It was now that he displayed his grasp of the importance of military intelligence. At a strategic level, his sources told him that Ambiorix had no desire to face him in a meeting engagement. The Gallic chieftain already had his plunder from the defeat of Cotta and Sabinus, and felt safe behind the sturdy earth and timber ramparts of his *oppidum* fortified tribal capital (this site yet to be identified). Evaluating this information, Caesar realized he now had the campaign initiative and acted accordingly. He interpreted his intelligence to show Ambiorix was overly reliant on his fellow Belgae Nervii allies and targeted them first, wiping them out. He then sought out the Eburones in their *oppidum*, taking his time to thoroughly scout their defences. This provided the tactical level intelligence to help accomplish a swift Roman victory. A massacre followed, with the ultimate fate of Ambiorix unknown.

Caesar then wintered in Cisalpine Gaul through to 52 BC, where he raised a new *legio* XIV to replace that lost and also created the new *legio*

XV. Given the size of his army now, and the scale of his butchery of the rebels in the previous campaigning season, he believed Gaul would now settle quietly into Roman provincial life. That was far from the case, and once more he was forced to fight another rebellion, that of Vercingetorix, king of the Arverni tribe. This he finally defeated at the Siege of Alesia in 52 BC, after which he announced all of Gaul finally pacified. Here again he used battlefield intelligence at both a strategic and tactical level to maximum effect. This proved a stark contrast to his later ignoring state-level intelligence in 44 BC prior to his assassination, as detailed in Chapter 3.

Even earlier, the first century BC historian Sallust credited much of Rome's success against the Numidians in the Jugurthine War in the late second century BC to the Roman leader Marius' meticulous military intelligence gathering operation at a strategic and tactical level after he took command in 107 BC. He says (*Jugurthine War*, 8.2):

> Marius acted with energy and discretion to survey with equal attention all aspects of his own and the enemy's situations from the beginning. He set about finding out the strengths and weaknesses of the two sides, he reconnoitred the movements of the king and anticipated their planning and traps, and he tolerated no slack on his side or security for theirs.

These and other contemporary examples show the importance placed on military intelligence by successful Roman commanders. With that established, I now turn to those who actually provided this function within the Roman military establishment. At a micro-level, in the Republic and Principate troops scouting immediately ahead of a campaigning force were styled *procursatores*, though these are not considered here given they were troops tasked from the ranks with this role rather than specialists. For that, I now turn first to the *speculatores*, and then the *exploratores*.

The *Speculatores*

The name *speculatores* originated with the Latin *specula* meaning watchtower or lookout post, a common term used across the empire. For example, in Roman Numidia two watchtowers built respectively by Commodus and Caracalla guarding the El Kantara gorge cut by legionaries of *legio* III *Augusta* through the Aures Mountains to link their legionary fortress at Lambaesis to a chain of vexillation forts along the Saharan fringe are called *burgi speculatorii* in contemporary epigraphy (Sheldon, 2005, 167).

The term first appeared in the context of military units in the mid-Republican period. Here, their key role was gathering tactical military intelligence, though as detailed their responsibilities greatly expanded over time. Such new roles included acting as military policemen (fully outside the various kinds of state-level policing set out in Chapter 3) and official state executioners on behalf of provincial governors, and as elite imperial guards, the latter over and above those detailed in Chapter 2. Note some commentators often refer to *speculatores* as spies. However, as I determine below, in their original role they were actually an extension of the tactical military intelligence gathering function of the mainstream military.

We have much insight into the activities of the early *speculatores* in the context of the various conflicts of the mid-Republican period. For example, when Polybius describes Scipio Africanus' discussions with the Numidian king Syphax in the winter of 204/3 BC at the climax of the Second Punic War, he details the Roman commander deployed *kataskopoi* to provide him with tactical military intelligence both before and during the encounter (Polybius, *The Rise of the Roman Empire*, 14.1.13). Most commentators translate the Greek *kataskopoi*, which references their intelligence gathering activities, as *speculatores* given the specifics of the information Polybius says they gathered. As Austin and Rankov detail (1995, 59):

> These talks were deliberately protracted to allow groups of experienced men, in disguise as attendants of the negotiators, the chance to look over the layout and construction of the Numidians' camp and later to contribute to a plan for attacking it at night.

Meanwhile, Caesar provides much detail of their use in the civil wars of the late Republic. For example, on one occasion the reputation of his *speculatores* as skilled scouts and gatherers of intelligence actually countered against him. This was during his 58 BC campaign against the Helvetii at the beginning of his conquest of Gaul when he found himself involved in intense negotiations with the Suebi king Ariovistus. To Caesar's surprise discussions continued into a second day and, suspicious this might be an ambush attempt that would put the Roman senior command at risk, he sent two junior officers instead of his usual negotiating team to continue the talks. One was a Gaul in Roman service, the other a Roman well-known to Ariovistus. The German king immediately suspected they were *speculatores* and put them in chains (*The Conquest of Gaul*, 1.47).

Later Caesar details the use of his *speculatores* when campaigning against the Belgae Nervii in northern Gaul in 57 BC, one of the most difficult campaigns in his Gallic conquests (*The Conquest of Gaul*, 5.49.8). Here, they were used to scout escape routes for his force out of a wide river valley where they had been fixed in place by a much larger Gallic army. These *speculatores* succeeded, allowing Caesar to slip away and later gather his entire army, he ultimately defeating the Nervii in the close run Battle of the Sabis.

Later, Mark Antony is well-known for a range of coins minted in their thousands which today numismatists call Anthony's 'legionary denarii'. Most were struck in the late 30s BC at Patras (Roman *Patrae*) in Greece and were used to pay his twenty-three legions and fleet ahead of his final, fateful campaign against Octavian that saw his ultimate defeat alongside Cleopatra VII at Actium in 31 BC. These coins are noted for their low silver content when compared to other contemporary Roman coins, this because they were minted in such numbers. Each range of coins minted by Mark Antony at this time features a dedication to a specific military unit. Crucially for this research, some of the units named were called *speculatores* and feature different types of standard to those depicted on the coins of normal legions (Cowan, 2014, 14). Indeed, it is within this range we have the only Roman reference to a specific *cohors speculatorum*.

Into the Principate, the primary sources continue to detail *speculatores* being used in specific campaigns. For example Tacitus (*The Annals*, 2.12.1) says Germanicus used them to provide detailed battlefield intelligence on the whereabouts of his Germanic opponents when campaigning along the Rhine in AD 16. The information they gathered enabled the Roman commander to deploy his troops in a particularly defendable location that proved vital to their eventual success.

Later, we have a fine Severan example of a leading *speculator* scouting officer. This is M. Oclatinius Adventus, appointed procurator in Britain by Septimius Severus at the beginning of the third century AD. Two inscriptions from this period detail his prior lengthy service leading units of *speculatores*, and it seems likely it was this experience that led to his deployment in Britain. Here, trouble was again occurring along the northern *limes*. Severus clearly needed a procurator skilled in gathering tactical military intelligence to help stabilize affairs.

In terms of gathering such intelligence, *speculatores* were also employed in a maritime capacity. This was in both the large, Mediterranean-based fleets of the later Republic, and the regional fleets of the Principate. For example Julius Caesar describes the use of *speculatoria navigia* vessels to gather intelligence during his Gallic campaigns (*The Conquest of Gaul*, 4.26), while some of Mark Antony's 'legionary denarii' coins which reference *speculatores* name maritime units and feature images of ships' prows.

In terms of command and control, *speculatores* performed their military intelligence gathering function in two ways, either directly serving a Roman military commander as an independent unit (note that early on they were often recruited directly from allied troops), or were specialist legionaries or (later) auxilia within a specific military unit. They gathered tactical military intelligence in a wide variety of ways. In the first instance, clandestine scouting ahead of the *procursatores* added an additional layer of battle-space detail to assist Roman commanders in their decision taking, as with Caesar when fighting the Nervii. However, they could also operate in a more clandestine role, this leading to them sometimes being called spies. By way of example, they are often described by contemporary sources disguising themselves as deserters or refugees to avoid interception by opposing scouts or security personnel. This was a tactic often used by *speculatores* to try to infiltrate an enemy camp, for example as attempted unsuccessfully by Metellus Scipio against Caesar in 46 BC prior to the Battle of Ruspina.

Speculatores as military policemen and executioners

As the Principate empire progressed, *speculatores* were also increasingly seconded to work in the governor's *officium consularis* as a specific new type of *beneficiarii consularis*. Here the *Historia Augusta* tells us they acted as what we today would call military policemen, this a totally different role to their original scouting function, they now tasked with ensuring the various entities making up the military establishment in a province were kept in line (*Pescennius Niger*, 3.6). Hodder, in his detailed study of the Roman army in Britain, helpfully provides detail in this regard, saying that by this time each legion was expected to provide ten such personnel to the governor for use in this new task (1982, 75). Fuhrmann adds that, in this military police capacity, they also provided the bodyguard for senior officials including the governor and procurator (2012, 193).

Though *speculatores* most often succeeded in this role, when they failed disaster followed. For example, Pertinax was sent to Britain in AD 185 by the emperor Commodus to quell a rebellion by all three legions in the province. The context was the trouble that had broken out there soon after the new emperor ascended the throne in AD 180, with the natives in the unconquered far north taking advantage of the imperial transition to breach Hadrian's Wall. Overwhelming the garrisons, they then headed south down Dere Street where they destroyed the fort and settlement at Corbridge (Roman *Coria*). In the process, they killed a Roman general and his bodyguard of auxiliary cavalry.

Commodus responded by ordering the British governor, Ulpius Marcellus, to counter-attack in force. His two-year campaign north of the border was a great success, with an inscription in Corbridge and two in Carlisle (Roman *Luguvalium*) referencing successful military action beyond Hadrian's Wall (Southern, 2013, 229). Commodus then received his seventh acclamation as *imperator* and took the title *Britannicus* in AD 184.

However, success came at a price. Given the large military presence needed to maintain the northern border in Britain, and its distance from Rome, the province had always proved troublesome, with the governor's *speculatores* military police always busy. Further, the three legions in Britain, *legio* II *Augusta* in Caerleon, *legio* XX *Valeria Victrix* in Chester and *legio* VI *Victrix* in York, were well-known for their volatility. In AD 180 Marcellus had already had to put down some kind of revolt in the legions, earning a reputation as a strict disciplinarian. Worse then followed after his victory in the north, with the legions breaking out in a full rebellion against him later in AD 184. Overthrown, he was recalled to Rome in disgrace, with the fate of his *speculatores* military police unknown.

The legions then tried to appoint a *legate* called Priscus as a usurper governor but he refused, with Dio (*Roman History*, 73.9) having him say 'I am no more an emperor than you are soldiers.' At this point Dio adds that the legions then appointed a delegation of 1,500 soldiers (he calls them 'javelinmen') to travel to Rome to denounce the Praetorian prefect to Commodus over some slight they felt he had caused them. However unlikely this sounds, it quickly prompted the emperor to restore order in Britain. First he ordered the *legates* of the three British legions to be cashiered, and then unusually replaced them with equestrian-rank officers promoted from within their own ranks (note *legates* in this period were always of Senatorial level, Kulikowski, 2016, 63). Commodus then, as a stopgap, appointed Marcus Antius Crescens Calpurnianus as a temporary governor. Birley (2005, 171) argues this may have been because, with the three legionary *legates* deposed, he may have been the only Senatorial-level aristocrat left in the province. Unsurprisingly, the Britons in the far north again decided to take advantage of the disruption and attacked the frontier again in early AD 185. However, they were once more defeated, with coins being minted to celebrate victory in Rome. This shows that although they were rebellious against the imperial centre, the three British legions were still willing to hold the northern *limes*.

Commodus now turned to his ultra-reliable imperial troubleshooter Pertinax to settle matters once and for all in Britain. Once in post as governor, Pertinax got to work straight away. His top priority was to bring the legions to heel, and like Marcellus he followed a very strict line in discipline. Again this seems to have backfired, for although he won over two of the legions, the other continued its mutiny. The *Historia Augusta* (*Pertinax*, 3.6) says the trigger was actually his turning down an offer to usurp Commodus. It says simply: 'They wished to set up some other man as emperor, preferably Pertinax himself.'

Whatever the cause, the mutiny was a serious event, the troops ambushing him and leaving him for dead, with his *speculator* bodyguards slain (Fuhrmann, 2012, 193). The *Historia Augusta* (*Pertinax*, 3.9) then says that when Pertinax recovered he punished the legion very severely, perhaps ordering a decimation whereby one legionary in ten was executed by his fellow soldiers. This seemed to work, with Dio (*Roman History*, 73.9) saying Pertinax eventually 'quelled' the mutiny. He then re-appointed *speculatores* from the legions to his *officium consularis* to ensure the ongoing loyalty of the legions to the imperial centre, and also to act as new bodyguards.

Fuhrmann also details that *speculatores* on the staff of the governor were also the official executioners of the provincial government (2012, 193). It is unclear if these individuals were standard *speculator* military policemen seconded to the *officium consularis*, or separately appointed middle-ranking officials.

We may have direct evidence of *speculatores* performing this role in Roman London. Here, the provincial capital's amphitheatre is located in the north-western corner of the city, immediately east of the Cripplegate vexillation fort. Built at the latest in the early AD 120s in its stone-built form (an earlier structure here was constructed in wood), this had a seating capacity of between 7,000 and 10,500 spectators. The amphitheatre was the place where public executions took place, with leading Roman London expert Perring saying (2917, 45):

> London is bound to have witnessed frequent executions, as the city held a pivotal role in Rome's administration of Britain, remaining under the direct command of the provincial governor (whose) judicial duties included imposing the death sentence and ordering public execution.

Evidence of this is highly visible in the archaeological record, where in the nearby upper Walbrook Valley and its tributaries hundreds of decapitated skulls have been found, these clearly the victims of deliberate beheadings (Elliott, 2021, 84). This region of Roman London was a highly suitable environment for the disposal of such deliberately unburied dead, or at least their skulls. It formed part of the city *pomerium* religious boundary, this an area favoured in the Roman world for the execution and burial of criminals. It was also in the north-west of the town, this a direction naturally associated with mortality beyond the setting sun, especially of an ex-judicial nature.

Further, we even have direct evidence of an individual *speculator* executioner in London. This is Celsus, a *speculator* seconded from Caerleon-based *legio* II *Augusta* whose later second century AD tombstone was found near Blackfriars Bridge (RIB 19). His funerary inscription shows he was responsible for judicial killing in the provincial capital, with his memorial now on display until recently in the Museum of London.

Meanwhile, *speculatores* on the staff of governors often had their own uniforms to identify them when on duty away from the provincial capital, much like the *frumentarii* detailed in Chapter 3. Funerary inscriptions of such *speculatores* also show them carrying 'Benefiziarierlanzen' spear-standards, a spear with a notably bulbous head used as a mark of office by various kinds of *beneficiarii*. Here, Austin and Rankov say (1995, 201): 'There can be little doubt that these spears marked these men out as officials of the governor, operating on his behalf and independently of any other military commander in the province.'

Similarly, some *speculatores* are also shown on epigraphy wearing a particular type of lance-badge attached to leather belts or straps on their uniforms, these also featuring a bulbous head. Examples in the archaeological record have been found in Britain, Germany and along the Danube.

Meanwhile, other epigraphic data also shows how such *speculatores* travelled when on official duty on behalf of the governor. While most tombstones show such officials standing alone, a well-preserved early third-century AD example from Belgrade shows a *speculator* in a fine carriage that bears his insignia of office (Sheldon, 2005, 144). Clearly, making an impression that projected imperial power was important when a *speculator* represented the governor around his province.

Speculatores as Imperial Guards

In the early Principate empire we also have a number of references to *speculatores* providing the close guard for the emperor himself, or his leading generals. These were mounted troops enlisted from within the Praetorian Guard who were completely distinct from the *equitatae* Praetorian cavalry, and recruited into a completely separate command structure reporting directly to the emperor.

Sheldon argues Augustus himself recruited the first *speculatores* guards from the Praetorians, not surprising since it was he who originally founded the guard (2005, 166). They are then referenced in the service of Tiberius when dispatched to inform governors and army commanders of his imminent demise (Tacitus, *The Annals*, 6.50.6), Claudius when protecting the emperor at dinner parties (Suetonius, *The Twelve Caesars*,

Claudius, 35.1), in the service of the 'Year of the Four Emperors' candidates Otho and Galba (Tacitus, *The Histories*, 2.11, and Suetonius, *The Twelve Caesars*, *Galba*, 18), and also protecting both Vespasian and Titus on the line of march when on campaign in Judaea during the First 'Great' Jewish Revolt in the late AD 60s (noting this was before either became emperor, *speculatores* being seconded by Nero, Josephus, *The Jewish War*, 3.6.2). Imperial guard *speculatores* finally disappear in the reign of Trajan, as do the Praetorian *equitatae* cavalry, with both replaced by the new *equites singulares Augusti*.

Given the number of imperial guard units already referenced in this book, the use of the term *speculatores* also in this role may seem confusing. However, we are most likely seeing a case of contemporary semantics, with the use of the word an ephemeral colloquialism for anything 'special' in a military sense during the first century of the Principate. Much the same, in fact, as we use the term special forces today.

The *Exploratores*

The name *exploratores* originates from the Latin *explorare*, meaning those who seek, explore or investigate (Cowan, 2021, 18). As detailed, the *exploratores* are best-known for their deep reconnaissance/strike and frontier surveillance roles in the Principate and Dominate phases of empire. Both roles feature the gathering of military intelligence, but this time of a more strategic nature.

A key issue here early in their history is the difficulty in the Republican period of separating their role from that of the *speculatores*. As Austin and Rankov say, at this time they seem to have been used to gather information in a very similar way to the latter (1995, 55). Sheldon agrees, saying the names *speculatores* and *exploratores* were often interchangeable at this time (2005, 164). By way of example, as detailed above, we have Caesar deploying his *speculatores* to find escape routes for his trapped army when fighting the Nervii in 57 BC. Here, the word he uses to describe their mission is *explorat*, even though the troops are specifically called *speculatores* (*The Conquest of Gaul*, 5.49.8). Aston and Rankov say this is most likely for euphonic reasons, but nevertheless the juxtaposition of the two terms is notable in this early period (1995, 57).

In terms of the Republican use of *exploratores*, while accepting these philological issues in this earlier period, we can again turn to Caesar for specific examples of their activities. Sheldon argues that most of Caesar's scouting and reconnaissance efforts were performed by *exploratores*, and the historical record shows this was indeed the case (2005, 210). For example, in his 52 BC campaign against Gallic rebels in Gergovia he specifically deployed *exploratores* on a reconnaissance mission to determine why his opponents had moved away from a defendable position (*The Conquest of Gaul*, 7.44.1).

Moving into the Principate, we now begin to see the *exploratores* increasingly used differentially to the *speculatores*, with the focus now on gathering strategic military intelligence. To start with a negative example, it is clear they dramatically failed in the case of Varus' disaster in the Teutoburg Forest in AD 9. Here three entire legions and their auxiliaries were lost while campaigning north of the frontier. This was in part caused by the native German *exploratores* in Roman service, tasked with deep reconnaissance in support of the legionary spearheads, being turned by Arminius and then leading the Romans to their doom.

The Romans made better use of more reliable *exploratores* in their subsequent punitive campaigns against the Germans, with for example Germanicus utilizing their deep reconnaissance skills to determine that his target in his AD 15 campaign, the Marsi tribe, were celebrating a religious festival. He therefore ordered an immediate strike from his base at Xanten (Roman *Vetera*) with 12,000 legionaries and 34 cohorts and squadrons of auxiliaries. His *exploratores* were then used again, this time to determine the quickest but most secure route to engage the enemy, which they did to great effect, enabling him to massacre the Germans (*The Annals*, 1.50.3).

In earlier research I argue we next see *exploratores* in action in the rescue of the Brigantian Queen Cartimandua in AD 69 (Elliott, 2021b, 90). Under her monarchy, this vast northern tribal confederation had long been an ally of Rome, especially after she had handed the leading native British resistance leader Caratacus to the Romans in AD 51. Having presented the emperor Claudius with the greatest exhibit of his conquests in Britain, the queen was rewarded with a formal alliance, and great wealth. With Roman control of Britain by this time edging northwards, broadly reaching a line from Chester in the west to The

Wash in the east, and with Roman attention turned to the sanguineous subjugation of modern Wales, the Brigantes were now an allied buffer state protecting the emerging Roman province to the south. However, all was not well, with Cartimandua divorcing her husband Venutius and replacing him with his armour-bearer Vellocatus. By AD 57, at a crucial time in the consolidation of Britannia, Venutius raised a Brigantian rebel army and declared war both on Cartimandua and her Roman sponsors. An initial Roman response with auxiliaries proved insufficient, and it took the deployment of *legio* IX *Hispana* by the governor Aulus Didius Gallus to defeat the rebels, with Cartimandua remaining on the throne.

However, the wily Venutius was not finished, and in AD 69 he took advantage of the turmoil across the Roman Empire as civil war erupted in the 'Year of the Four Emperors'. Here he staged another revolt, this time with the help of allied and unconquered tribes from the far north, and once more Cartimandua's position was in peril. She again appealed to the Romans for support, but the governor Marcus Vettius Bolanus had no legions available, these perhaps unreliable at the time given the crisis back in Rome. He therefore sent a flying column of troops northwards who managed to extract Cartimandua back to safety within the borders of the province to the south. Later, larger formations of Roman troops then campaigned further north in Brigantian territory, with the poet Statius (*Silvae*, 53 - 56) having Bolanus campaigning in the 'Caledonian Plains'. While they failed at this point to remove the Brigantian usurper Venutius from power, this event focused Roman attention on the far north of Britain for the first time proper, and within a decade much of Brigantian territory up to the Solway Firth–Tyne line had been incorporated into the Roman province (Elliott, 2021b, 102).

Focusing back on Bolanus' daring rescue of Cartimandua in AD 69, this is clearly a prime example of a Roman world special operation. One should note the distances involved which the Roman extraction force had to travel, and in enemy territory too. The Brigantian capital was located at modern Aldborough in North Yorkshire (Roman *Isurium Brigantum*), some 120km north of the then frontier. The obvious assets that Bolanus had to turn to here were his *exploratores*, this a classic example of their deep reconnaissance/strike role. Indeed, this was an operation so audacious it brings to mind Skorzeny's Operation Oak glider-borne rescue of Mussolini in September 1943. Further, if the *exploratores* led a mixed force including regular auxiliary cavalryman, another modern analogy would be the 1976 Entebbe Raid where the Israeli Sayeret Matkal counterterrorist unit led a combined arms operation featuring other elite regulars.

Later in Britain, Tacitus then details that in AD 83, a hard-pressed Agricola used his *exploratores* to guide him and his relief force deep into enemy territory to rescue the hard-pressed *legio* IX *Hispana* who were in danger of being over-run in their marching camp in the far north (*Agricola*, 26.1). Notably, this is the last time we hear of this legion in contemporary history.

Meanwhile, Cowan (2021, 20) argues that the twenty-five auxiliary troopers from *cohors* I *Hispanorum* detailed in a roster led by a centurion and a Decurion across the Danube during Trajan's Second Dacian war (AD 105–106) were also seconded *exploratores*, while later as the war reached its conclusion the senior officer Tiberius Claudius Maximus of *cohors* II *Pannoniorum* led a picked troop of mounted *exploratores* in a bid to capture Decebalus, he only failing when the Dacian king cut his own throat. Nevertheless, Maximus finished the job, hacking the king's head off to present to Trajan.

Back to Britain, once the northern frontier was formalized along the Solway Firth–Tyne line in the reign of Domitian at the end of the first century AD, and later fortified under Hadrian in the AD 120s, we begin to see specific epigraphic and literary evidence of *exploratores* units operating in the far north of Britain in the early second century AD. This shows three were based at the forts at High Rochester (Roman *Bremenium*), Risingham (Roman *Habitancum*) and Netherby (Roman *Castra Exploratorum*). Astonishingly, the latter appears to have actually been named after its *exploratores* incumbents (Bishop, 2014, 51). It is from around this time that we can also see the *exploratores* beginning to perform their role as frontier guardians, using bases such as these.

Meanwhile, a prime example of *exploratores* in their deep reconnaissance/strike role can be seen in the campaign of Maximinus Thrax against the Alamanni on the Rhine frontier in AD 235, the year he became emperor. This was an immense undertaking, he driving his legionary spearheads an astonishing 600km beyond the Rhine deep into Germania if one believes the primary sources (clearly an exaggeration, but still indicating an impressively deep penetration). Here they would have forged ahead of the main strike forces, ensuring routes were clear of ambushes, identifying fordable crossing points of major rivers and targeting the local economy to deny supplies to the local natives. Further, wherever possible they would have worked to prevent the coalescence of critical mass by any enemy warriors gathering to challenge the Romans. As Cowans explains, Maximinus was well served by his *exploratores* in the region, with contemporary sources indicating a large number were available, these organized into various *numeri* (2021, 20). This is an interesting term to use given it was associated with non-regular forces at this time, enlisted outside the normal Roman military recruitment process. However, the larger units were still commanded by senior Roman officers. We have a specific example of one such commander in the region at this time, an equestrian called Titus Flavius Salvanius who was the prefect of the *exploratores Divitienses* unit based at Mainz (Roman *Moguntiacum*) on the Rhine frontier where the inscription on his tombstone details his service.

Meanwhile, a fellow *exploratores* officer in the region at this time set up a monument in fulfilment of a vow to a local deity (interestingly, not a deity from the Classical pantheon) which references the *numerus exploratorum Germanorum Divitiensium Alexandrioano-rum*. This was paid for out of the *numeri*'s own funds, with Victorinus being the unit's *cornicularius* senior clerk (Cowan, 2021, 20). Another *exploratores* officer in the region at the time was Titus Flavius Romanus, a legionary centurion from *legio* II *Primigenia*, on secondment to lead the *exploratores Sturi* unit who are recorded helping reconstruct the bath house at Walldurn.

Maximinus also used his *exploratores* to good effect at the end of his short reign, this time against the imperial centre when in AD 238 he was approaching north-eastern Italy through the Julian Alps. This followed the Senate in Rome switching its allegiance to the North African usurpers Gordian I and II earlier in the year, and later after their demise at the hands of Maximinian loyalists to the leading Senators Pupianus and Balbinus (Scarre, 162). Knowing that a hastily gathered army might be waiting for him to block his route as he approached from the north-east, his *exploratores* ranged far and deep ahead of his advance and were soon in Italy proper where they reported his line of advance clear all the way to Aquileia at the head of the Adriatic Sea. Here, a Maximinian advance force had earlier made a lightning strike, cutting their way through to the key port city but then failing to take it, they lacking the siege machinery to storm its walls. Maximinus therefore approached with his full force, including the slow siege train, hence his need for the *exploratores* to ensure the way was clear. This they did well, though sadly all to no avail for him given during the subsequent siege his troops mutinied and assassinated him.

Cowan argues that many *exploratores* were recruited directly from native peoples along imperial frontiers, for example Germans or those of German lineage along the Rhine (2021, 210). By way of example, a Merovingian tomb excavated in Heidelburg in 1901 contained five Roman gravestones, one of which was that of an *exploratory* called Respectus whose father was called Berus, a Suebian name meaning 'bear'. However, other *exploratores* could be recruited directly from the ranks of the mainstream military. The *cohors* XX *Palmyrenorum* auxiliary unit presents a fine example, this a *cohors equitata milliaria* mixed infantry and cavalry unit originally recruited from Palmyra in Roman Syria. When first raised in the second century AD it initially served in Dacia, before being posted back to the eastern frontier. Relevant here, while stationed on the Danube a fragmentary roll-call roster shows ten cavalrymen and five infantrymen seconded to serve as *exploratores*. Meanwhile, other specific *exploratores* units raised from the legions and auxiliary units along the northern and southern *limes* are recorded in epigraphy found at *Tsanta* in modern Bulgaria, Alt-Kalkar (Roman *Burginatium*) in Germany and at *Albulae* in Mauretania Caesariensis in modern Algeria (Austin and Rankov, 1995, 191). Here, the units are termed *numeri exploratores*, this organizational nomenclature reflecting that of the *speculatores* (see below). Other inscriptions referencing *exploratores* found along the Rhine add the term *divitienses*, showing these were based as regulars at the fortress of Deutz (Roman *Divitia*) on the right bank of the Rhine opposite Cologne. This was an ideal location to allow the *exploratores* based there to strike north and east into Germania when tasked with deep reconnaissance/ strike missions, or to range deeply into enemy territory when helping secure the frontier.

Over and above their role providing a deep reconnaissance and strike function, Spiedel argued that several units of *exploratores* were specifically raised in the field to act as the spearhead unit for a main legionary strike force (1983, 63). They then, he suggests, reverted to become standard *exploratores* units after the end of a given campaign. In his research he identified one individual he believed actually commanded such a unit based on an early third century AD Greek inscription, this T. Porcius Cornelianus who held several auxiliary commands before becoming the *praiphektos exploratoron Germanias* commander of the German scouts.

While, as detailed, units of *exploratores* could be organized on an ad hoc basis when required, most were formed into *numeri*. Sadly we have no idea how large these units were, though Sheldon argues convincingly they were larger than their *speculatores* counterparts given their respective roles, with the latter operating in smaller, more clandestine detachments (2005, 166). Further, *exploratores* seem to have had a more formal organizational structure given they were often based alongside *beneficiarii* when deployed away from the provincial centre, a good example being found at Risingham (Austin and Rankov, 1995, 203).

We do have more clarity on how *exploratores* were expected to operate than we do for *speculatores*, based on contemporary commentary. For example, Vegetius provides great insight, saying (*Epitome of Military Science*, 3.6):

- They should play very close attention to mapping out routes of advance in enemy territory.
- They should ensure maximum security well in advance and on the flanks of the main strike force when advancing in enemy territory.
- They should keep a keen eye out for anything that looks suspicious while advancing in enemy territory.
- When possible, they should operate at night.

Other contemporary sources also suggested *exploratores* operate in native dress, or use camouflage.

Closing Discussion

In my research for this book I have frequently come across references to *speculatores* being the Roman equivalent of modern special forces. However, if one objectively engages with the data, it is clear that in their scouting role they were effectively an extension of the Republican and Principate *procursatores* given they maintained their umbilical link with the military formation they were operating in support of.

Meanwhile, in their 'spying' role the tasks they performed were simply a variation on those undertaken by the *frumentarii* and (later) the *agentes in rebus*. If we set them against the special force criteria detailed in Chapter 1, at certain times they did go through a demanding selection procedure, were sometimes used to secure operational advantage, and occasionally (though not often) may have been deniable. However, they were not trained in normal circumstances for non-regular warfare. Therefore, I would argue there is not enough collective evidence to suggest that, on a regular basis, the scouting and 'spying' *speculatores* were special forces as we determine them today, but rather specialists at gathering tactical military intelligence in the field. In their other roles, either as military police, executioners or imperial guards, they were certainly not special forces.

Meanwhile, at least during the Principate, we are on much firmer ground with the *exploratores* when considering whether they were special forces or not. By this time there was a clear distinction between their activities and those of the *speculatores*, with their clear focus of gathering strategic level military intelligence. Further, we have far more primary source data to work with. This shows them playing a key role as the empire expanded, they providing invaluable service in their deep reconnaissance and strike role. Multiple examples above show how this function was fully integrated into the Roman strategic military planning process. Later, as the empire's frontiers began to settle, their security role along the wide-ranging *limes* became even more important, though note even then this was based on deep penetrations into enemy territory.

Once more, here we can set our Roman candidate service against the special force criteria detailed in Chapter 1. Certainly there was a demanding selection procedure to join an *exploratores* unit as a commander or trooper. Such warriors were expected to operate deep in enemy territory, independent of any umbilical with the main campaigning force they were supporting, or well away from their base if providing frontier defence. Next, the *exploratores* were also trained in non-regular warfare techniques, with frequent references to them using special skills acquired for a given mission. They also had a real *esprit de corps* that I think comes through in the many examples of epigraphy on funerary stele and in other inscriptions. This all allowed them to help the main campaigning force when on the offensive to secure operational and strategic advantage, and similarly assisted the defence of the *limes* by disrupting enemy offensive operations and providing intelligence deep from within the enemy interior. Finally, when required, I also believe the activities of the *exploratores* could be deniable, especially when using native troops, or operating at night or in disguise. Therefore, based on these criteria and the data I have set out, I believe that the *exploratores* are our first candidate service that we could class as Roman special forces.

I close this chapter with a brief reference to *equites legionis* legionary cavalry given some believe they were either *speculatores* or *exploratores* rather than the legionary scouts and messengers as usually described, for example by Connolly (1988, 217). These warriors are certainly an enigma, given the cavalry function in later Republican Roman armies was provided by allied troops, and in Principate imperial armies by auxilia. Only one key reference mentions them in the traditional role detailed above, this Livy who records the legionary cavalryman Tiberius Sempronius Gracchus reconnoitring a route and then delivering a message during the Second Macedonian War (*The History of Rome*, 37.7). Further, the usual number attached to each legion also only comes from one contemporary source, this Josephus (*The Jewish War*, 3.120). However, most references to legionary cavalry indicate their role was very different, and of the 'special' variety. For example Josephus details how Vespasian asked for elite volunteers from among his *equites legionis* to lead the final assault against the walls of Jotapata in the First 'Great' Jewish Revolt (*The Jewish War*, 3.254). Therefore, the hypothesis that they were actually *speculatores* or *exploratores* does have a ring of truth about it, though sadly we have no definitive data in the historical or archaeological record to support this.

Chapter 5

Protectores

By the later third century AD, as the 'Crisis of the Third Century' transitioned towards its close, a new elite Roman troop type emerged. These were called *protectores*, they usually referenced as members of a new senior officer pool at court, or imperial guardsmen. However, as with the *speculatores*, the meaning of the name changed over time to cover a variety of specialist warriors. Some of these are Roman special forces candidates, as I detail below.

The *Protectores Domestici*

The term *protectores* first appeared in the reign of Gallienus, co-emperor with his father Valerian from AD 253 to AD 260, and then alone after the latter's shocking demise at the hands of the Sassanid Persians through to AD 268. For much of his reign as solitary emperor Gallienus faced multiple challenges as he struggled to stop the empire from fracturing irrevocably. These included the breakaway Gallic Empire of the usurper Postumus in the west, and Gallienus being forced to rely on the Palmyran king Odaenathus to secure his eastern frontier. While maligned by some, Gallienus faced his struggles stoically. Indeed, it was he who continued the process begun by Septimius Severus of transforming the Principate military establishment he had inherited into something that, through the later reforms of Diocletian and Constantine, was very different by the time of the later Dominate.

In the first instance he reformed its command structure, effectively democratizing it. Earlier, Severus had for the first time appointed equestrian-level aristocrats to command the three Parthian legions he had raised, *legio* I, II and III *Parthica*, instead of the usual Senatorial-level *legatus legionus*. Now Gallienus went further, replacing all Senatorial-level legionary commanders with equestrians. From this point onwards the old Senatorial *legati* completely disappear, replaced by new commanders styled either *praefectus legionis vir egregious* or *praefectus legionis agens vice legati*. To qualify for the position an equestrian had to have extensive front-line experience, this including holding the post of *primus pilus* (the most senior centurion in a legion) twice. As Kean and Frey say (2005, 141): 'Under Gallienus the final barriers separating lower from higher command were abolished, and any man who attained the centuriate could now rise to the very highest levels of command.'

Gallienus later went even further in these reforms, removing the rank of *tribuni laticlavii* from the legionary command structure. These had been the junior Senatorial officers being groomed for later legionary command.

Meanwhile, beset on all sides as Rome's opponents sought to take advantage of the demise of Valerian in the east and rise of Postumus in the west, Gallienus realized the Principate military system based on legions deployed in legionary fortresses around the frontiers of empire wasn't fit for purpose. He therefore decided that a more flexible system was required. At the point he became sole emperor, he only had one legion deployed as a strategic reserve, this *legio* II *Parthica* which Severus had based at Albanum, 34km from Rome, to keep an eye on the political classes there (Elliott, 2016, 156). He also knew that his heavy infantry-based legions were increasingly suffering at the hands of opponents deploying heavy shock cavalry and mounted bowmen. This was nothing new for the Romans, well used to fighting Parthians in the east, and later the Sassanid Persians who replaced them. Similarly, the Sarmatians had long been a threat along the Danube frontier. However, now multiple new threats featuring mounted opponents shaped Gallienus' thinking, he creating a series of all-cavalry reserve forces based at multiple locations deep within the empire (MacDowall, 1995, 4). These could be deployed rapidly to deal with any breach of the imperial frontier as required.

The first such force was established in AD 260 shortly after his father's capture by the Persians, this being based in Milan under the command of an equestrian called Aureolus (later to turn against Gallienus after a fall from grace, he then siding with Postumus). Others were later based in Greece and Syria. These new cavalry reserve formations were soon in action when, for the first time, large-scale Gothic and Heruli mounted raiding parties penetrated deep into the Balkans interior in the mid AD 260s, sacking Athens in the process. Gallienus went on to make extensive use of his cavalry reserves, their importance shown by the standing of their commanders who were given equal rank to a Praetorian prefect.

Gallienus' new cavalry reserve also featured new types of mounted warrior for the first time. The basic unit of organization was now the *vexillatio* commanded by a tribune, this broadly tracking the administrative structure of earlier auxiliary units, with three *ordines* of two centuries each, giving a total complement of 600 horsemen. The basic cavalryman remained the *eques*, with the same panoply as their earlier Principate forebears. However, they were now supported by specialist types including *equites contariorum* armoured lancers and *equites cataphractarii* cataphracts. The latter were fully armoured, both man and horse, the rider wearing a suit of armour called *lorica plumata* which covered the entire body, and a substantial helmet including a gilded face plate. Meanwhile, new types of light cavalry including *equites illyriciani* armed with javelins and bow equipped *equites sagittarii* also began to appear. These new types were joined later in the century by other specialist cavalry types, including *equites clibanarii* armoured lancers also equipped with bows, *equites dalmatae* who were armed in a similar way to the *equites illyriciani* (their names indicating where they were initially recruited from), *equites mauri* who were based on their Moorish *symmachiarii* predecessors and who were much in demand when fighting the Sassanid Persians, and finally *equites scutarii* who may have been regular bodyguard cavalry.

With reform of the military command structure and institution of his new cavalry reserves both complete, Gallienus next turned his attention to his own personal security. Realizing the foreign policy challenges he faced were impacting on domestic stability, he knew his regime was at risk. He was also aware that, based on their past actions, the Praetorian Guard and other guard units he'd inherited (including the *equites singulares Augusti*) were untrustworthy. He therefore decided to transform an institution he'd earlier established into a new, independent guard unit based within his court, as opposed to externally as with the Praetorians. The original body were called the *protectores divinis lateris*, this founded around AD 260 to award promising centurions with a position in the imperial staff college. Kean and Frey (2005, 143) argue this was part of Gallienus' process of democritizing the military leadership, his aim being 'to counteract the lack of education among the centurions that increasing "barbarisation" of the army had produced.' This proved a masterstroke at first, providing Gallienus with an ultra-loyal cadre of officers from whom to select those destined for future high rank. We may also have an indication here of his ultimate intention for this new group given the Latin name translates literally as 'imperial body guard' (Austin and Rankov, 1995, 212).

Whether intended or not, this soon became apocryphal as, by the end of Gallienus' reign, at least some of his *protectores divinis lateris* were being styled *protectores domestici*, these now providing the emperor's close bodyguard at court. One can only imagine the friction this caused with the Praetorians and *equites singulares Augusti*, it being no surprise that Gallienus was eventually assassinated in September AD 268. However, the *protectores domestici* survived his death and went on to be proved one of the later empire's most enduring institutions, operating alongside Constantine I's *scholae palatinae* after his disbandment of the Praetorian Guard and *equites singulares Augusti*.

It is unclear if all the earlier *protectores divinis lateris* transferred to the new *protectores domestici* role, or whether the junior officer cadre remained in being, with those deemed most capable and loyal further promoted to protect the emperor as *protectores domestici*. The latter seems the most likely, though the reality is we will probably never know given the myriad of titles given to various court functionaries by this time, as evidenced in previous chapters.

Amazingly, a recent archaeological find has provided great insight into the life of one *protector demosticus* who served as a guardsman for Diocletian at the beginning of the fourth century AD. This was found in 2017 in the north-western Turkish town of Izmit (Roman *Nicomedia*) when the regional authority was building a new office block. Archaeologists from the Kocaeli Museum of Archaeology and Ethnography were appointed to carry out a rescue excavation of the site in advance of the new construction and quickly found that beneath it lay an extensive Roman necropolis, with the burials there dating from the second to the fourth century AD. They then worked over a two-year period to systematically excavate the whole site, eventually finding five in situ sarcophagi, fifty-one tile tombs and two cremation burials in amphora.

One of the former in particular stood out, a high-quality stone sarcophagus featuring well-preserved images of warriors and, most importantly, a lengthy inscription detailing the deceased as Tziampo (or

Ciampo), a native of the province of Dacia Minor in the *diocese* of Moesiae. At the time of his death he was a *protector* in the service of Diocletian, the emperor having earlier established *Nicomedia* as his Tetrarchic capital in the east. The key visible text on the inscription provides much detail, saying:

> To the spirits of the dead! I am Tziampo, protector of the divine flank. I lived 50 years. I do not allow anyone except my son Severus or my wife to be buried in this tomb. I served nine years as a trooper in the cavalry, 11 years as a cavalry officer, and ten years as a protector. If anyone dares to bury another in this tomb, he will pay 20 *folis* (a Roman bronze coin, devalued heavily by Diocletian) to the *fiscus* (the imperial treasury) and 10 to the city treasury.

The imagery on the sarcophagus also features clues to Tziampo's earlier career. For example, the warriors shown are cavalrymen spearing fallen foot opponents with long *contos* lances. If these represent Tziampo then they indicate he served with an *ala* of *equites contariorum* armoured lancers. Meanwhile, in terms of human remains, two burials were found in the sarcophagus. Based on the grave goods, one was Tziampo and the other likely his wife, this only the eighth such interment that mentions the incumbent as a *protectores domestici*.

Various additional roles are also ascribed to the *protectores domestici* over and above providing the emperor's close bodyguard. For example, Sheldon says that some were specialists in gathering intelligence, this a crowded field by this time, while others were used to monitor religious and ecclesiastical affairs, to keep an eye on provincial authorities, inspect *fabricae* state armament manufactories, and act as the emperor's enforcers and executioners. In this latter role they perhaps replicated the provincial duties of some *speculatores*, but at an imperial level (2005, 265). Two good examples of *protectores* acting in this role occurred in the reign of Claudius Constantius Gallus, elder half-brother of Julian and eastern *caesar* under his cousin Constantius II from AD 351 to 354. In the first instance, the paranoid *caesar* had his *protectores domestici* arrest an aristiocrat at court (then located at Antioch-on-the-Orontes) who he thought had been insolent in his presence. The offender was quickly executed. Then, realizing the man's influential son-in-law had fled on hearing the news,

Britain's Special Air Service remains the best-known special forces unit in the world today. Seen here shortly after their creation, operating in North Africa early in the Second World War. (*Public domain*)

Colourised image of Otto Skorzeny, the leading German special operations leader in the Second World War. (*Bundesarchiv, Bild 183-R81453*)

Israeli commandos from the Sayeret Matkal counter-terrorist unit return after the Operation Jonathan raid to rescue hostages from Entebbe, Uganda in 1976. (*Public domain*)

The *speculatores* played a key role in Gaius Julius Caesar's conquest of Gaul, particularly in his 57 BC campaign against the Belgae. (*Public domain*)

Mark Antony was well-known for his 'legionary denarii' coin issues struck in the late 30s BC to pay his twenty-three legions and fleet ahead of his final campaign against Octavian. These included specific coins minted featuring legions, *speculatores* and, as here, the fleet. (*The British Museum via Wikimedia*)

Roman emperors of the Principate relied on the Praetorian Guard for their close protection when in Rome and on campaign. They often proved fatally unreliable and were finally disbanded by Constantine I. (*Carole Raddato via Wikimedia*)

Maximinus Thrax, first Roman emperor in the 'Crisis of the Third Century', who used *exploratores* to support his campaigns against the Alamanni on the Rhine frontier in AD 235. (*Capitoline Museums/public domain*)

Roman legionaries in *testudo* formation and riverine naval craft carrying out amphibious operations during the Marcomannic Wars in the later second century AD. Marcus Aurelius, Lucius Verus and Commodus all made use of *speculatores* and *exploratores* in this conflict.

Tombstone of Celsus from the western cemetery in Blackfriars, London. A legionary from *legio* II *Augusta* seconded to work on the governor's staff as a *speculator*. Spy, military policeman, executioner, or all three.

Unarmoured Roman troops shown on a stone slab found at the Antonine Wall fort at Croy Hill. Some believe these may represent *exploratores*.

Groma in the legionary fortress of Lambaesis, home to the *exploratores* operating in the Aures Mountains in Roman North Africa.

Naval scouts, likely *speculatores* or *exploratores*, were used by Julian the Apostate in the AD 350s on the River Rhine as part of his campaign against the Alamanni. Here a recreation of a monoreme cutter of the *Classis Germanica*.

The Multangular Tower in York, part of the Dominate-period defences of the legionary fortress there behind which the *Dux Britanniarum* and his surviving *limitanii* sheltered during the AD 367 'Great Conspiracy'.

Eagle in the Snow. Severan temple viewed through the Arch of Caracalla in Djemila, modern Algeria. Here excessive taxation helped ferment the rebellion of Firmus which saw Count Theodosius deploy *exploratores* in the region.

Ruins of the Roman fort and *colonia* at Tabuda on the Saharan fringe, modern Algeria. The campaigning theatre for the end game of Firmus' revolt.

Throughout the Roman occupation in Britain there was no love lost between the Roman military and the native Britons of the far north. This was frequently represented in contemporary Roman sculpture which was designed to send a very specific message to the locals. Here a lion pounces on a lamb in this fountain head from Corbridge (originally a decoration on a mausoleum), and the Cramond Lioness from the Firth of Forth devours a native. In both cases it is very clear who the Romans are meant to be. It was in this hostile environment that the *areani* operated.

The Saxon Shore fort at Portchester where one of the last *exploratores* units ever mentioned is detailed in the *Notitia Dignitatum*.

An *equites legionis* legionary cavalryman, who some believe may have actually been *speculatores* or *exploratores* rather than the legionary scouts and messengers as usually described. (© *Graham Sumner*)

Gallus sent his *protectores* to track him down. They captured him in Armenia from where he'd hoped to travel to Constantinople, killing him before he could send a petition to Constantius II (Ammianus Marcellinus, *The Later Roman Empire*, 15.3.7).

Constantius himself also often had cause to use his *protectores domestici* in the same role as his popularity plummeted due to an increasingly onerous regime. One example in AD 354 was in the context of a dinner party held in Sirmium by Africanus, the governor of Pannonia Inferior in the *diocese* of Pannoniae. Here Ammianus Marcellinus provides vivid detail, saying (*The Later Roman Empire*, 14.7.12):

> Amid these dire aspects of trials and tortures there arose in Illyricum another disaster, which began with idle words and resulted in peril to many. At a dinner-party given by Africanus…certain men who were deep in their cups and supposed that no spy was present freely criticized the existing rule as most oppressive; whereupon some assured them, as if from portents, that the desired change of the times was at hand; others with inconceivable folly asserted that through auguries of their forefathers it was meant for them.

Unbeknownst to them, one of the guests was actually a leading member of the *agentes in rebus* who promptly reported the event to Constantius. Soon, two *protectores domestici* were despatched to arrest all those present at the dinner party, including the host Africanus. Many were then executed, some in the arena. Here we get a unique historical snapshot of two branches of the late Roman security services operating together, the *agentes in rebus* and *protectores domestici*.

However, and crucially for this research, our primary sources also indicate some *protectores domestici* were also tasked with carrying out special operations, often behind enemy lines. Here we therefore have the first thread that might indicate some *protectores domestici* could be Roman special forces candidates. This is a hypothesis I will now test for the remainder of this chapter.

Protectores in Action

We have detailed contemporary accounts of *protectores domestici* carrying out special operations for the emperor, both in written history and epigraphy. In particular, Ammianus Marcellinus provides unique insight given his lengthy career in the service.

One of the earliest accounts to survive is a petition by an officer called Flavius Abbinaeus sent to the emperors Constantius II and Constans in AD 341. This was a papyrus document found in Egypt and recounts his past exploits in imperial service. This includes a key event when he was ordered to accompany a high-ranking officer called Senecio in escorting a senior delegation of Blemmye refugees to the imperial court at Constantinople in AD 338. The rank of his superior gives an indication of the importance of this mission, he styled the comes *limitis Thebaidos Superioris* meaning he was responsible for the Egyptian *limes* in Upper Thebaid, Rome's most southerly frontier. There they faced the never-conquered native Blemmye, a nomadic tribal people whose kingdom existed from around 600 BC through to the sixth century AD in Nubia. The Blemmye proved a major nuisance to Roman Egypt, often raiding the upper Nile region through Upper Thebaid. Although not a particularly sophisticated opponent in terms of their tactics and technology (most were unarmoured bowmen, though they did occasionally use African forest elephants), the size of their armies often proved problematic for the region's incumbent legion, *legio* II *Traiana Fortis*. The Romans countered this Blemmye threat with a series of fortifications and watchtowers built to protect the rich agricultural land in the Nile Valley.

On arrival in the eastern capital the court was so impressed with Abbinaeus' service that he was immediately promoted into the *protectores domestici*, and then tasked with a special mission. This was to escort the now-completed mission of Blemmye refugees back deep into their Nubian homeland. The party travelled with a large military escort which clearly performed its task well given there is no indication their return was obstructed after they had crossed the frontier. Interestingly, it appears Abbinaeus' return mission took at least three years, indicating he stayed in Blemmye territory for a significant period of time before returning back across the *limes* (Austin and Rankov, 1995, 225). On his return he then rejoined the emperor's *protectores domestici* who by this time were stationed in *Hierapolis* in south-western Anatolia where the court had relocated. Also of interest, when he arrived there Abbinaeus had with him a large number of Blemmye warriors who were promptly recruited into the eastern imperial army.

Reading between the lines, here perhaps we see a skilful imperial troubleshooter who caught the eye of major influencers at court when he initially arrived with Senecio, the latter's mission most likely bringing leading Blemmye nobles to petition the empire for support at home. Abbinaeus' promotion to the *protectores domestici*, and then special mission to escort the delegation back home, shows this request was successful, with the result an overall foreign policy victory for Rome and a beneficial outcome for Abbinaeus' career progression.

However, the most famous *protector domesticus* is our most important source for much of the Dominate, Ammianus Marcellinus himself (Austin and Rankov, 1995, 19). By this time in the mid-fourth century AD it was common for *protectores domestici* to be seconded by the emperor to work on the staff of senior military officers. These included the *magister equitum* in charge of mounted troops in late Roman *comitatenses* field armies, the *magister peditum* in charge of foot troops, and the *magister militum* in overall command. All three positions granted the holder close access to the emperor at all times, making them very powerful individuals in their own right. It is in this context we see Ammianus seconded by Constantius II to serve with his *magister equitum* Ursicinus on the eastern frontier in the early AD 350s shortly after promotion into the *protectores domestici*. Here Ammianus carried out a number of special operations across the eastern *limes* in Sassanid Persian territory, though we have little detail except he operated as a representative of Ursicinus, rather than being physically with him (Austin and Rankov, 1995, 229). This shows Ammianus was clearly considered a safe pair of hands dealing with delicate foreign policy issues, especially given the fragile situation on the eastern frontier at the time.

Here, the great Shapur II had earlier won a major victory against Constantius in AD 348 at the Battle of Singara, and then only just failed to capture Nisibis after a long siege. This was the key frontier city that gave access from Persian controlled Mesopotamia into the heart of Roman Syria. Its fall would have opened the way for the Persians to invade the rich and densely-populated Roman Levant.

More promisingly in terms of specific insight regarding the *protectores domestici* in action, one of Ammianus' later missions when serving with Ursicinus provides much more detail. This was in AD 355 when they were sent by Constantius, now based in Milan, to deal with the rebel Silvanus in Cologne, his usurpation detailed in Chapter 4 in the context of the *agentes in rebus*. This was a serious, if somewhat unfortunate given the series of misunderstandings involved, challenge to the emperor on the northern *limes*. Constantius' response is important here given the light it sheds on the day-to-day operations of the *protectores domestici*. In the first instance, Ammianus details the composition of the senior military team sent on the mission, saying (*The Later Roman Empire*, 15.5.2):

> ...the officer who had brought the news to Milan was ordered to depart with some tribunes and ten of the *protectores domesticii*, together with some guards as an escort to aid him in the discharge of his public duty. And of these I myself was one of the *protectores domesticii*, along with my colleague Verrinianus; and all the rest were either friends or relations of mine.

Unpacking this, the officer arriving at court with the news was likely Ursicinus himself given the gravity of his intelligence. The tribunes Ammianus mentions included senior members of the *agentes in rebus* and also *notarii* to record events so that a legal evidence trail was available to support the actions of the delegation. The domestic guard, which Ammianus later says were included at Ursicinus' specific request, were likely a contingent of *scholae palatinae*.

Next Ammianus describes the journey to Cologne, clearly made in haste using forced marches in fear that news of Silvanus' revolt would spread. He says (Ammianus Marcellinus, *The Later Roman Empire*, 15.5.2):

> And now all of us, fearing mainly for ourselves, accompanied Ursicinus a long distance on his journey; and although we seemed as exposed to danger as gladiators about to fight with wild beasts, yet considering in our minds that evils are often the forerunners of good, we recollected with admiration that expression of Cicero's, uttered

by him in accordance with the eternal maxims of truth, which runs in these words:

> And although it is a thing most desirable that one's fortune should always continue in a most flourishing condition; still that general level state of life brings not so much sensation of joy as we feel when, after having been surrounded by disasters or by dangers, fortune returns into a happier condition.' Accordingly we hastened onwards by forced journeys, in order that the *magister equitum*, who was eager to acquire the honour of suppressing the revolt, might make his appearance in the suspected district before any rumour of the usurpation of Silvanus had spread among the Italians. But rapidly as we hastened, fame, like the wind, had outstripped us, and had revealed some part of the facts; and when we reached Agrippina we found matters quite out of the reach of our attempts.

On arrival in Cologne Ammianus details the reception they received, noting the local elites and military were clearly supporting Silvanus' usurpation. Also, for the first time, we get real insight into the clandestine nature of Ursicinus' mission. His orders were to convince the usurper he was leading an embassy to him on behalf of Constantius, though in reality their orders were to do away with Silvanus without inflaming the situation with the military any further. Of note, this shows enough troops in the north supported Silvanus at the beginning of his revolt to stop Constantius quickly gathering a field army to counter the rebellion. He therefore had to revert to diplomatic subterfuge, if only to buy time to gather a large enough military force. Ammianus provides much detail here, saying (*The Later Roman Empire*, 15.5.2):

> For a vast multitude of people, assembled from all quarters, were, with a mixture of haste and alarm, strengthening the foundations of Silvanus's enterprise, and a numerous military force was collected; so that it seemed more advisable, on the existing emergency, for our unfortunate general to await the intentions and pleasure of Silvanus, who was assuring himself by ridiculous omens and signs that he was gaining accessions of strength. By permitting his feelings of

security to increase, by different pretences of agreement and flattery, Silvanus, it was thought, might be relieved from all fear of hostility, and so be the more easily deceived.

Ammianus then says that at first Ursicinus found it difficult to balance the diplomatic ruse while seeking a clear opportunity to remove Silvanus. Specifically, the *protector* says (*The Later Roman Empire*, 15.5.3):

> But the accomplishment of such a design (the subterfuge) appeared difficult. For it was necessary to use great care and watchfulness to make our desires subordinate to our opportunities, and to prevent their either outrunning them, or falling behind them; since if our wishes were allowed to become known unseasonably, it was plain we should all be involved in one sentence of death. However, Ursicinus was kindly received, and the very business itself forcing us to bend our necks, having been compelled to prostrate himself with all solemnity before the newly robed caesar, still aiming at higher power, was treated as a highly favoured and eminent friend; having freedom of access and the honour of a seat at the royal table granted to him in preference to every one else, in order that he might be consulted with the more secrecy about the principal affairs of state. Silvanus expressed his indignation that, while unworthy persons had been raised to the consulship and to other high dignities, he and Ursicinus alone, after the frequent and great toils which they had endured for the sake of the Republic, had been so despised that he himself had been accused of treason in consequence of the examination of some slaves, and had been exposed to an ignoble trial; while Ursicinus had been brought over from the east, and placed at the mercy of his enemies; and these were the subjects of his incessant complaints both in public and in private.

Based on Ammianus' narrative here, Silvanus was completely taken in by Ursicinus' diplomatic smoke screen, which was surprising given the Frank was a seasoned military leader well-used to the darker side of Roman court politics. One theory is that his false sense of security derived from the supposed loyalty of the Rhine troops given their previous support for

Magnentius, the earlier usurper in north-western Europe who had been very popular with the military.

With Silvanus' guard down, Ursicinus and his party got to work. Soon they discovered the Rhine legions were urging Silvanus make a power play for the western throne itself and fully usurp Constantius. Ammianus says (*The Later Roman Empire*, 15.5.3): 'While, however, he was holding this kind of language, we were alarmed at the murmurs of our soldiers, the troops showing every eagerness to make a rapid march through the defiles of the Cottian Alps.'

The imperial party was now fearful events might overtake them and decided to take a risk. This involved bribing some of the legionaries to become agitators against Silvanus in the hope this would turn enough troops against the usurper to bring about his end. Here, Ammianus shows they were clearly aware of the level of jeopardy they faced, saying (*The Later Roman Empire*, 15.5.3):

> In this state of anxiety and agitation, we occupied ourselves in secretly deliberating on the means of arriving at our object; and at length, after our plans had been repeatedly changed out of fear, it was determined to use great industry in seeking out prudent agents, binding them to secrecy by solemn oaths, in order to tamper with the Gallic soldiers whom we knew to be men of doubtful fidelity, and at any time open to change for a sufficient reward.

Ammianus finally explains, again in great detail, how the gruesome coup de grâce was carried out, he saying (*The Later Roman Empire*, 15.5.3):

> Therefore, after we had secured our success by the address of some agents among the common soldiers, men by their very obscurity fitted for the accomplishment of such a task, and now excited by the expectation of reward, at sunrise, as soon as the east began to redden, a band of armed men suddenly sallied forth, and, as is common in critical moments, behaving with more than usual audacity. They slew the sentinels and penetrated into the palace, and so having dragged Silvanus out of a little chapel in which, in his terror, he had taken refuge on his way to a conventicle devoted to the ceremonies of the Christian worship, they slew him with repeated strokes of their

swords. In this way did a general of no slight merit perish, through fear of false accusations heaped on him in his absence by a faction of wicked men, and which drove him to the utmost extremities in order to preserve his safety.

With matters settled and Silvanus dead, Ursicinus then returned to Milan with his imperial entourage, once more resuming his position at court. He was next in frontline action back in the east in the late AD 350s when trouble flared again along the frontier with Sassanid Persia. Ammianus, by now a senior *protector domesticus*, accompanied Ursicinus and was again in the thick of things. He provides vivid detail about the negotiations that took place between Constantius and Shapur II in early AD 359, and it is highly likely he was actually present at some of their meetings in person. In this capacity, he also had access to the extensive records of the senior *notarii* who accompanied Constantius, even detailing a famous letter sent by Constantine I to Shapur at the beginning of the latter's reign in AD 310 (*The Later Roman Empire*, 17.5.3-9).

Relations between Rome and Persia on the eastern border had become increasingly fractious as the AD 350s progressed, and when the direct talks between Shapur and Constantius failed war broke out (Kean and Frey, 2005, 201). Here Ammianus is highly critical of the Roman emperor after he placed Ursicinus, his most experienced commander, under the command of Sabinianus, the *magister peditum* of the east. The two generals famously didn't get along, resulting in a lack of coordination between the *comitatenses* field army under Sabinianus and the *limitanii* border troops in Roman Mesopotamia and Osrhoene under Ursicinus.

Amid these operational issues Ammianus was sent on his first mission of the war, to make contact with Jovinianus, the satrap of Gordyene located south of Lake Van in the upper Tigris Valley. This was the most westerly Persian province. Jovinianus was a former hostage in Rome and known for his Roman sympathies. Having reached the regional capital at Nisibis, Ammianus then tells us Jovinianus warned him of the approach of the main Persian invasion force, led by Shapur himself. The satrap promptly sent him with a local guide to a nearby mountain top. From this high vantage point Ammianus saw the vast Sassanid army grinding its way towards them 80km away. Though this seems an improbable distance, it does indicate how large the Sassanid army was. With this vital intelligence Ammianus promptly headed back to court to report his news, with Ursicinus then ordering the *dux* army commander in Roman Mesopotamia and its civilian *praeses* governor to adopt a scorched earth policy to slow the Persian advance (*The Later Roman Empire*, 18.6.21). The *magister equitum* then headed east himself to oversee the building of new frontier defences, taking Ammianus with him.

Shapur initially had the upper hand in the war and succeeded in capturing both the recently fortified city of Amida and the fortress of Singara (where the Romans had earlier been defeated in set-piece battle in AD 348) in north-western Mesopotamia. Ammianus himself was present at the siege of the former and provides forensic detail of the Roman defence which included sallies by legionaries which set fire to the Persian siege lines. However, after an outbreak of plague Roman resolve faltered and eventually Shapur's much larger force managed to force their way into the city. Ammianus and two other *protectores* managed to escape, famously attaching a helmet to a rope made from ripped clothing to slake their thirst from a deep well while crossing an arid region dotted with reeking sulphur springs (*The Later Roman Empire*, 19.8.8).

Although the Romans quickly regained both Amida and Singara, their initial loss infuriated Constantius who promptly sent Ursulus, his *a rationalis* chief financial minister, to view the damage in Amida. He was highly critical of the army's defence there, Ammianus quoting him as saying (*The Later Roman Empire*, 20.11.5): 'Look at the courage with which the cities are defended by our soldiers, for those whose salary bills the wealth of the empire is already barely sufficient.'

The military leadership didn't forget this slight and after Constantius' death in November AD 361 Ursulus' trial and execution were one of the key demands made by the senior generals at court for supporting Julian the Apostate, the new *augustus*. Meanwhile, in later AD 359 poor morale in the eastern army in the wake of such imperial dissatisfaction may also explain the failure of Constantius' main counterthrust into Sassanid territory which was quickly repulsed. The war then reached a stalemate as both sides eyed each other warily across the restored frontier, with Ursicinus' career a late casualty after Constantius dismissed him despite his long and loyal service. Ammianus now briefly seems to have stepped back from his role in the *protectores domestici*.

It was at this moment Constantius sent his famous dispatch to Julian in Paris (Roman *Lutetia*), the latter his western *Caesar* and still basking in the glory of his mighty victory over the Alamanni at the Battle of Strasbourg in AD 357. In the note he ordered Julian to send reinforcements to the eastern front (Kean and Frey, 2005, 201). The scale of those the *augustus* demanded Julian send gives some idea of the casualties his field army and *limitanii* had suffered in the recent conflict with the Persians. It included 300 men from every unit under Julian's command, plus four full units of Gallic and Frankish *foederates*. This put Julian in a difficult position given he'd promised many of his Gallic legionaries and *auxilia palatina* they would never have to serve in the east. Thus, when the *caesar* put Constantius' demand to them they refused point blank, and then promptly declared him *augustus*. This created an immediate schism with Constantius, dragging the *augustus* back west with a huge army to confront the upstart Julian. On the way he died on 3 November AD 361 at the ancient city of *Mopsuestia* in Cilicia in south-eastern Anatolia, declaring Julian his rightful successor on his deathbed.

Only the huge losses suffered by Shapur in AD 359 stopped the Persian king renewing his war against Rome when Constantius' attention turned west. Julian, aware that Shapur's allies were also wavering, decided to take the initiative once emperor, and in AD 363 launched an enormous offensive deep into the Sassanid heartland. This set the scene for Ammianus to reprise his role as a troubleshooting *protectores domestici*, with Julian recalling him to the colours.

The detail Ammianus provides here of Julian's campaign is of the highest order. For example, early on he describes the Persian army drawn up in battle formation under the command of Merana, the leader of the Sassanid cavalry, its most important arm. The battleline included fully-armoured cataphracts, lancers, horse archers and war elephants (*The Later Roman Empire*, 25.1.10). Ammianus also spent time while campaigning with Ormizdas, the Sassanid prince and elder brother of Shapur who had fled his country and taken refuge in Roman territory. He actually served in the Roman army in the AD 363 campaign, with Julian clearly aiming to set him on Shapur's throne after the victory he expected.

Ammianus also provides detail of the various places Julian's campaign travelled through as it ground its way down the Euphrates Valley on the way to the Sassanid capital of Ctesiphon. He actually names most of the Persian strongholds, for example giving precise information on Coche, formerly the Hellenistic city of Seleucia. There he describes a palace 'constructed in the Roman fashion…' that featured a large, verdant hunting park stocked with exotic wildlife for the Shapur to hunt when resident (*The Later Roman Empire*, 24.5.1-2).

The highpoint of Julian's campaign was his great victory at the Battle of Ctesiphon on 29 May where he defeated the Persian army before the city walls. However, he was unable to take the well-fortified Sassanid capital and was forced into a humiliating retreat back to Syria, this time along the Tigris Valley. Harried all the way by Persian cavalry, especially horse archers, the emperor was killed by an arrow at the Battle of Samarra while unwisely engaging an enemy ambush without his armour (Browning, 1978, 243). This left the Roman army trapped between the valleys of the Tigris and Euphrates, with Julian's successor Jovian (AD 363–AD 364) forced to make a humiliating peace with Shapur in exchange for safe passage back to Roman Syria. Ammianus is scathing about this agreement, which saw the Romans surrender much of their territory east of the Tigris, together with Nisibis and Singara. Shapur then turned his attention to the north and soon conquered Armenia, with the Romans unable to intervene (*The Later Roman Empire*, 25.6.15).

Ammianus remained in the *protectores domestici* after Julian's death, accompanying Jovian on his retreat until they reached Antioch-on-the-Orontes. There he resigned his post for a last time, and was still resident in the city in AD 372. He later moved to Rome where he died around AD 400.

Organization of the *Protectores Domestici*

We have no details of the title held by the commander of Gallienus' original *protectores divinis lateris*, but we do for the *protectores domestici*. By the early fourth century AD the post holder was being styled the *Comes Domesticorum*. This was a very important posting, the holder playing a key role in the emperor's *consitorium*, this the new Dominate replacement for the earlier Principate *Consilium Principis* main advisory council as originally created by Augustus.

In terms of recruitment, the early *protectores domestici* were recruited directly from Gallienus' original *protectores divinis lateris* officer cadre, with most former centurions marked out for imperial favour. However, as with other special force candidate units we have considered to this point, their later recruitment opened up to other military personnel (as with Flavius Abbinaeus and Ammianus Marcellinus), and even civilians with the required skill set and loyalty to the sitting emperor (Austin and Rankov, 1995, 225).

Meanwhile, while we have no specific detail about how the *protectores domestici* were organized, it is noteworthy that their role involved front line combat when required. We have already mentioned Ammianus Marcellinus participating in the defence of Amida against Shapur, while earlier the future emperor Galerius had served as a *protector* in a military capacity after an earlier career in the *equites scutarius*. We even have detail of *protectores domestici* who died while on duty. These include the fourth century AD Valerius Valentus whose funerary epigraphy specifies he 'fell in civil war in Italy...', and one Viatorinus who died 'in *barbarico*...' fighting the Franks. Therefore, it seems reasonable to argue that the *protectores domestici* were organized along the same lines as Constantine I's *scholae palatinae*, who were also front line fighting troops.

Closing Discussion

The *protectores domestici* were clearly special in that they were, among other things, elite guard troops who served alongside other late Roman guard units and intelligence-gathering personnel at court, and elsewhere when the emperor or various senior *magisters* deployed to the empire's frontiers. However, in my above research we have only three examples where they were clearly operating well beyond the frontiers of Roman territory, with Flavius Abbinaeus in the lands of the Blemmye, Viatorinus fighting the Franks and Ammianus Marcellinus accompanying Julian. Most often, they were operating either within the empire, or along its borders. Therefore, while they were clearly volunteers or recruits, they may have been trained for irregular warfare, and may have been deniable, they were not (at least regularly) used to secure operational and strategic advantage outside imperial territory. Consequently, I believe they are not special forces as we would define them today, but rather elite Roman troops similar to those detailed in Chapter 2.

Chapter 6

Areani and Later Roman Special Forces

The Roman military establishment in the Dominate phase of empire was dramatically different to that of the Principate. The legions based around the borders of the empire were long gone, replaced with *comitatenses* field armies positioned deep within the imperial interior, and *limitanii* gendarmes who policed the frontiers. Further, the balance in most armies on campaign had altered dramatically in favour of mounted troops. Even when heavy infantry did play a key role, the legionaries were less capable than their Principate predecessors. Now, more often than not, the key line-of-battle troops were *auxilia palatina*, recruited en masse from German and Gothic confederations along the Rhine and Danube, and from Isaurian tribes in the Anatolian interior.

However, at least initially, there was one area of continuity. This was with regard to three of the special force candidates considered earlier, namely the *speculatores*, *exploratores* and *protectores*. The latter, as a purely late-empire phenomenon, have already been considered in full in their own chapter. The former two though, after a largely anonymous 150 years in the historical record, reappear again in the mid-fourth century AD. In Chapter 4 I concluded that while the *speculatores* were not special force candidates, the *exploratores* were. I now re-evaluate that here to see if this had changed, in either case, by the time of the later empire.

Further, by this time many other types of specialist and elite troop types had also begun to emerge across the empire. One group in particular are my final special force candidate. These are the *areani* in Britain, and by way of analogy, elsewhere in the empire. In telling their story I also provide background detail about later Roman Britain to set the scene for their activities, which ultimately proved so problematic for the imperial centre.

Speculatores in the Later Empire

By the later Dominate period, at a time when new specialist units like the *agentes in rebus*, *notarii* and *protectores* had appeared, the *speculatores* re-emerge in the historical record. The first late example occurred in AD 354 when *speculatores* played a key role in Constantius II's response to a major Isaurian insurgency (Austin and Rankov, 1995, 56). Here, they warned the regional authorities that a rebel warband was advancing towards the Pamphylian city of *Seleucia* on the Mediterranean coast of modern Turkey. This allowed defences to be set in place to protect this major urban centre, with the rebels then moving on empty-handed. Interestingly, the *speculatores* here were operating as covert agents among the local population, a task usually ascribed at this time to the *agentes in rebus*, rather than in their earlier role gathering tactical military intelligence in support of a campaigning force in the field.

Ammianus Marcellinus then reports a succession of incidents where *speculatores* again played an important role in the east. Given his proximity to many of these events, particularly through his extensive service as a *protector domesticus* there, he is a first-class witness. In the first instance he details a Roman deserter on the eastern frontier in AD 359 as the conflict there fizzled out who he calls a *speculator* in Persian service (*The Later Roman Empire*, 24.5.2). Next, he says that while Constantius II was based at Edessa in AD 361 shortly before he set off to deal with the usurping Julian, he sent his own *speculatores* to gather intelligence on the intentions of the Sassanid Persians across the *limes* to ensure his rear was secure before he travelled west (*The Later Roman Empire*, 25.1.1). This was in the context of the stalemate along the eastern frontier after the inconclusive war with Shapur II. Interestingly, Ammianus says the reports sent back to court by the various *speculatores* in the field, and also through intelligence gathered from interrogating refugees, proved so contradictory that it was useless. Here once more we have references to *speculatores* gathering covert intelligence, they operating independently among local communities in disguise, rather than fulfilling their earlier more military-focused role.

Ammianus next references *speculatores* in AD 365 when the usurper Procopius used them to support his doomed bid for the eastern throne (*The Later Roman Empire*, 25.1.1). Context is important here, so I briefly detail Procopius' life to that point. He was born in AD 326 in the town of

Kizkalesi (Roman *Corycus*) in Cilicia on the south-eastern Mediterranean coast of modern Turkey. From early in his life, Procopius was well connected at court, being a maternal cousin to Julian the Apostate and with his second wife Faustina the widow of Constantius II. His brief rise to power set a trend for the family which lasted a century, with the leading fifth century AD Roman general Procopius his grandson and the western emperor Anthemius his great grandson.

Procopius' early career at court set him on course to fully understand the importance of intelligence gathering and special operations. He was quickly promoted from the ranks of the mainstream military into the *notarii*, and as a senior tribune in the corps took part in Julian the Apostate's AD 363 campaign in Sassanid Persia as one of the emperor's senior advisors. As the Roman forces advanced towards Ctesiphon he was then promoted to become a *comes*, one of the highest ranks in imperial service, and together with the *comes rei militaris* Sebastianus put in charge of the upper Tigris region with 30,000 men (*The Later Roman Empire*, 23.3). This was the theatre reserve for the advancing Roman legionary and auxiliary spearheads to the south, and also served as the main logistics base for the Roman campaign. Procopius was also tasked with maintaining good relations with the Armenian king Arcases II. Soon, as Julian struggled to capture the Sassanid capital, Procopius and Sebastianus were ordered to join the emperor in the south with fresh troops and supplies. However, their advance was delayed by poor weather. By the time they joined the main Roman army at Thilsphata between Nisibis and Singara it was already in retreat, with Julian dead.

Shortly afterwards Procopius met the new emperor Jovian, his fall from grace following almost immediately. Ammianus, who says his story was based on the first-hand account of Procopius' friend and leading Senator Strategius Musonianus, explained this was because of a baseless rumour spread at court in the aftermath of Julian's death. This said he'd ordered his kinsman Procopius to take the throne if he died on campaign. Fearing retribution from Jovian, especially given a similar rumour had already caused the execution of the army commander Jovianus, Procopius went into hiding (*The Later Roman Empire*, 25.9). However, this proved short-lived and he was soon back in imperial service, tasked with supervising Julian's funeral in Tarsus. Ammianus then says Procopius retired to

Kayseri (Roman *Caesarea Mazaca*) in central Anatolia with his family to live a private life.

Zosimus also details the same event, even providing a little more detail (*New History* 4.4.1). Here, Julian gave Procopius a purple imperial robe, explaining his actions only to the *comes* in a private audience. Then, when Jovian was acclaimed emperor, Procopius requested an audience where he gave the new emperor the robe and revealed to him Julian's private message, that he Procopius should succeed Julian. Fearful for his life, he then asked Jovian to be allowed to retire from public life, which the new emperor accepted. It is worth noting here the power Procopius had at court given his senior role as a *comes*, and as a former senior *notarii*. Using a modern colloquialism, he knew 'where all the bodies were buried'. Clearly Jovian, fearful that Procopius may have set in place an insurance policy in the event of an untimely death, wanted Procopius out of the way and quiet. Zosimus then repeats Ammianus' description of Procopius retiring to live privately with his family in Kayseri, with no mention of the *comes*' involvement in the transport and burial of Julian's body.

I turn again to Ammianus for the next development in Procopius' colourful later career, this again in the context of imperial succession. After Jovian's death in February AD 364 the new emperors Valentinian I and Valens quickly turned on him given the rumours of Julian's earlier plans to elevate Procopius, despite him retiring from public life. In particular, Valens in the east felt threatened and was well-known for his vengeful nature (Kean and Frey, 2005, 212). The new emperors decided to act swiftly and sent troops to arrest Procopius, the wily *comes* surrendering without fuss but asking if he could first dine with his family one last time. The soldiers agreed, indeed joining in the feasting, but while they were enjoying their wine Procopius seized the opportunity to flee with his family northwards. Reaching the coast of Bithynia, they then crossed the Black Sea to hide in the Greek-speaking cities of the Crimea (then called the *Tauric Chersonese*), moving from one to another to stay ahead of the imperial spies looking for them. However, Procopius clearly didn't enjoy the experience, given Ammianus has him 'living the life of a wild beast and skulking in rough country...' (*The Later Roman Empire*, 26.6).

After a while Procopius grew tired of being on the run and decided to fight back. Returning to northern Anatolia, he made for *Chalcedon*. This was a major city in Bithynia, now an Asian suburb of Istanbul, where his old friend Strategius lived. Together they now plotted a usurpation against Valens, the eastern emperor very unpopular given a huge increase in taxation. Here he had been badly served by his *a rationalis* chancellor who also happened to be his father-in-law Petronius. The former commander of a military unit called the Martenses (Ammianus calls it a legion, though it is later listed in the Notita Dignitatum as a *limitanii* unit), Petronius had a reputation for greed and avarice (*The Later Roman Empire*, 26.6). Soon he was chasing overdue taxes dating back as far as the reign of Aurelian in the early AD 270s. The shrewd Procopius sensed an opportunity and now began to make clandestine visits to Constantinople, his covert activities aided by his unkempt and emaciated appearance. Here, in addition to his recent deprivations, he was clearly using the skills he'd learned gathering intelligence as a member of the *notarii*.

It is now that the *speculatores* appear in Procopius' story because, as a first step in gaining the support of the eastern army, he subverted those working on the eastern imperial staff. These then began spreading false rumours about Valentinian I and Valens in Constantinople, insinuating Petronius was planning to increase taxes even further. With the tax burden already onerous, rioting broke out in the streets.

Procopius then ordered the *speculatores* to direct his disinformation campaign specifically at the military garrison in the region, which Ammianus says comprised the Tungicani and the Divitenses legions (*The Later Roman Empire*, 26.6). These were normally deployed on the Danube frontier. Their presence near Constantinople shows Valens was already expecting trouble. However, his precaution backfired when both, at the prompting of Procopius' *speculatores*, switched sides.

Now, with the regional military behind him as well as the intelligence service, Procopius proclaimed himself emperor on 28 September AD 365, quickly taking control of the *dioceses* of *Thraciae* and *Pontica* (Cornell and Matthews, 1982, 172). However, the key *diocese* of *Asiana* stayed loyal to Valens and, after an initial crisis of confidence when he almost made terms with Procopius, the sitting emperor fought back. Here he was supported by his Praetorian Prefect (and famous Neoplatanist author) Saturninius Secundus Salutius, and also the veteran general Flavius Arintheus. Valens then won two closely fought battles against Procopius at *Thyatira* in Lydia and *Nacolia* in Phrygia. Beaten, the usurper then fled again, hiding in mountainous Phrygia in the hope he could escape north and across the Black Sea again. However, his *speculatores* now turned on him and convinced his two leading generals, Agilonius and Gomarius, to betray him to Valens in return for a pardon. Procopius was then quickly captured, and then executed by Valens on 27 May AD 366 in the most brutal way. First, his body was tied fast to two trees. These were then bent down in separate directions. When released, Procopius was ripped apart. This was a means of execution usually reserved for bandits in the region, the shocking event designed to warn off any other would-be challengers for the throne. Things also didn't end well for Agilonius and Gomarius, with Valens reneging on his pardon and having them sawn in half.

Of note here, once more we have the *speculatores* performing a completely different role to that of their forebears in the Principate. In each reference by Ammianus, instead of providing tactical military intelligence to a campaigning force, they were once more operating akin to the late empire's *agentes in rebus* and *notarii*.

Speculatores are finally mentioned by Ammianus in the context of Valens' doomed campaign against Fritigern's Gothic confederation that ended in the disaster at Adrianople in AD 378. Here, after control of the northern Balkans had been lost, the emperor had to rely on his *speculatores* to provide intelligence about the whereabouts of the various Gothic columns operating in the region. To do this they wore disguises, mixing with the Goths and their followers, many of whom were former slaves who had fled the estates where they had been forced to labour. This provided the good quality intelligence that allowed Valen's *magister peditum* Sebastianus to successfully raid the main Gothic camp. Here the Romans recovered much of the booty Fritigern had stored to that point in his campaign (*The Later Roman Empire*, 30.11). Once more, however, here the activities of the *speculatores* again reflect those of the *agentes in rebus* and *notarii*, gathering local intelligence through clandestine means in what was effectively a domestic setting.

Exploratores in the Later Empire

The *exploratores* also reappear in the historical record in the mid-fourth century AD, and again a changing role is evident, though not immediately. Early on, they still maintained their deep penetration role, providing strategic military intelligence as an armed reconnaissance asset. Later, however, reflecting developments elsewhere in the Roman military, they became far more sedentary.

In the first instance, when the *protector* Ammianus was active on the eastern frontier in AD 359, he details being guided by a centurion over trackless terrain deep into enemy territory while scouting Shapur II's army to gather intelligence about its strength and capabilities (*The Later Roman Empire*, 24.5.1). Cowan argues convincingly the centurion was an *explorator* from a frontier scouting unit (2021, 20).

The *exploratores* are next referenced, again by Ammianus, in the context of the rebellion of the Numidian Berber prince Firmus in North Africa in AD 373. Firmus was the son of a senior *legate* in the western army called Nubel who was also a key figure in the Christian church in North Africa. Nubel had amassed great wealth and when he died Firmus killed his half–brother Zammac, accusing him of stealing his inheritance. Unsurprisingly, this quickly attracted the attention of the *vicarius* in charge of *Africae*, the regional *diocese*. Sadly for Firmus he was a friend of the now dead Zammac and soon moved to arrest Firmus. However, the latter knew the *vicarius* was unpopular, with a reputation for protecting the rich cities in the region from raiding Berber tribes only after they had paid him a substantial bribe. Those particularly affected included Constantine, Djémila (Roman *Cuicul*) and Timgad (Roman *Colonia Marciana Ulpia Traiana Thamugadi*). Firmus, with an eye for the main chance, decided to risk all and led a revolt which lasted two years.

Initially, Firmus proved highly successful given he went to great lengths to ensure the support of the local church and nobility. However, given the importance of the grain supply from this hugely fertile region to Rome, the emperor Valentinian I was forced to intervene. Knowing how popular Firmus was, he sent his key imperial trouble-shooter. This was Flavius Julius Theodosius (often called Theodosius the Elder, or *comes* Theodosius), a remarkable soldier of Spanish birth whose second son later became the emperor Theodosius the Great. The older Theodosius had earlier made his name defeating the 'Great Conspiracy' insurgency in Britain in AD 367 when styled the *comes Rei Militaris per Britanniarum* (see later in this chapter for full detail).

Arriving at Cherchell (Roman *Caesarea*), capital of the province of *Mauretania Caesariensis* on the Mediterranean coast of modern Algeria, Theodosius received word that Firmus was ready to compromise and was on the verge of reaching an honourable settlement with the emperor. It is here Theodosius' *exploratores* now appear in the story, warning him that Firmus was actually plotting to assassinate him. It is unclear if these were troops who had accompanied his field army to North Africa, or were locally based. Whichever it was, Theodosius reacted on their intelligence with characteristic speed, personally interrogating the local magistrates he suspected of being in league with Firmus. Under duress they confirmed the story was true and he quickly moved to arrest Firmus. However, the rebel was tipped off and fled south to the Aures Mountains on the Saharan fringe, here obtaining support from the local Berber tribes. This presented Theodosius with the prospect of a protracted guerrilla war against these elusive opponents from the Numidian interior, this similar to the previous insurgencies of Jugurtha and Tacfarinas centuries earlier. However, Theodosius was highly experienced in such conflict and mounted a lightning offensive southwards with a fast column of cavalry and specialist light infantry, led by his *exploratores* who were clearly gathering strategic-level military intelligence on the way, much like their Principate forebears. These troops drove Firmus over the mountains into the Sahara proper where the rebel leader fled from one tribe to another ahead of the Roman pursuit. Finally, the Isaflenses tribe decided to challenge the Romans in return for a huge bribe from Firmus.

After an inconclusive battle where the Isaflenses king Igmazen fielded 20,000 troops, and in which Firmus tried to convince the Romans to desert and hand over Theodosius in return for another bribe, the Isaflenses had a change of heart and arrested Firmus. However, the usurper managed to strangle himself before the Romans could take charge of him. His body was then tied to the back of a camel and taken north-eastwards by Theodosius to Setif (Roman *Sitifis*), capital of the province of *Mauretania Sitifensis*, and there shown the local nobility to prove the revolt was finally over (Hughes, 2013, 131).

To this point the *exploratores* of the later empire were acting exactly as had their Principate forebears. However, as we move towards the turn of the century, things begin to change. For example, six units of *exploratores* are recorded in the *Notitia Dignitatum*, with their role clearly very different. These are listed under the command of three *duces* and one *comes*, the latter with only *limitanii* otherwise under his command (Austin and Rankov, 1995, 237). This is interesting in itself given that, while *dux* are usually associated commanding such border troops, *comes* most often commanded *comitatenses* field armies (Elliott, 2020a, 170). This firmly anchors the *exploratores* in this very late phase of the Dominate on the borders of the empire rather than aggressively scouting ahead of armies on campaign, as in the earlier empire. Additionally, there is no data to show them carrying out deep penetrations in their new defensive role either, as did the earlier *exploratores* along the *limes* of the Principate. Here, finally, we have the *exploratores* passively guarding the borders of the empire, a role most still associate them with to this day.

Of the *exploratores* units detailed in the *Notitia Dignitatum*, four were based in key forts on the south bank of the Danube at *Novae*, *Taliata* and *Zmirna* in modern Bulgaria under the *dux* of *Moesia Prima*, and at Tekija (Roman *Transdierna*) in modern Serbia under the *dux* of *Dacia Ripensis*. The first three were all located very close to the Iron Gates, a very narrow gorge on the Danube that controlled access to the upper river. Meanwhile, nearby Tekija is historically a key crossing point on the Danube, used for example by Trajan in his two early second century AD Dacian campaigns. Its importance is shown by the location of a twin fort on the north bank of the Danube, this occupied earlier in the Principate by vexillations from *legio* XIII *Gemina*. This north-bank fort was still occupied in the later Dominate when the unit of *exploratores* was based opposite to the south.

Of interest, it is unusual to have four units of *exploratores* based so close together, with Austin and Rankov suggesting they may have originally been one larger unit, this then divided to find accommodation in these relatively small forts for a specific operation, and then remaining there (1995, 238). They further speculate that, given their longevity in the region at these forts, by the very late fourth century AD they may have lost their 'special' status.

The final two units of *exploratores* listed in the *Notitia Dignitatum* were based in Britain, with both *numeri*. The first was based at Bowes (Roman *Lavatris*) in North Yorkshire under the command of the *Dux Britanniarum*, this the late Roman commander charged with defending the northern frontier with a number of *limitanii* units. Meanwhile, the second was interestingly based at Portchester (Roman *Portus Adurni*) on the south coast under the command of the *Comes Litoris Saxonici per Britanniam*. This is the famous Count of the Saxon Shore, a title which today gives us the name Saxon Shore fort for those fortifications situated around the south east coast of Britain. Portchester on the Solent is the most easterly. Austin and Rankov argue that these two units were most likely two of the *exploratores* formations earlier detailed resident at Netherby, Risingham and High Rochester as detailed in Chapter 4 (1995, 238).

That based at Portchester is the most thought provoking given its maritime location. By this very late stage of the Roman occupation of Britain, the Count of the Saxon Shore only commanded *limitanii* given many of the *comitatenses* field army troops had already been deployed to Gaul through usurpations originating in Britain, or to bolster the defences there more broadly. Why a unit of *exploratores* was based on the south coast of Britain is open to question given their usual role, at this late stage, was the protection of land frontiers. We do have references to naval scouts (not specifically called *speculatores* or *exploratores* in the primary sources) being used by Julian the Apostate in the AD 350s along the Rhine as part of his campaign against the Alamanni, though these actually fulfilled the traditional *exploratores* role of deep penetration armed reconnaissance. Here they campaigned deep into Alamanni territory ahead of Julian's main incursions north of the Rhine (Elliott, 2021b, 172). However, that was clearly not the role of the *exploratores* at Portchester. There, as with troops posted at all of the Saxon Shore forts, the garrison had a purely defensive role, doing no more than deter nearby raiding in the coastal littoral. In this they clearly failed, given Britain fell out of official Roman control at the beginning of the fifth century AD. Of further interest, Austin and Rankov also highlight that by the AD 420s this unit of *exploratores* in Portchester had relocated to Gaul where they are listed serving under the *magister equitum per Gallium* (1995, 238).

The final mention of *exploratores* again comes from the *Notitia Dignitatum* where, in the early fifth century AD, a unit in Thrace is detailed having been split into separate vexillations. Based on the available data, these are specifically not those detailed above based around the Iron Gates or Tekija on the Danube frontier slightly earlier, but a separate unit based deeper within imperial territory. From here the vexillations were well placed to assist the imperial defence against deep penetrations into imperial territory by Goths and Huns, though note that again this was a purely defensive role and a far cry from the activities of earlier *exploratores*.

The *Areani* and Later Roman Britain

I now detail our last Roman special force candidate, the *areani*. As they are specifically a late Roman phenomenon in Britain, here I embed their story in the narrative of this *diocese* as it approached the end of official Roman control here in the early fifth century AD. However, note they also provide a useful analogy for other similar specialist troop types based around the frontiers of the late empire.

Our key source is again Ammianus Marcellinus, and the picture he paints is of an increasingly grim situation in Roman Britain as it began its final spiral of decline. As Max Adams says (2020, 36):

> The general theme is of military crisis and usurpation, before a dramatic curtain fall in the first quarter of the fifth century AD. Cut to Gildas, writing some time in the later fifth century AD or early sixth century AD, recording a woeful picture of abandoned cities, civil war and invasion by the impious tribes of Germania. Bede copied him, and more remote chroniclers of the Britons concurred.

The fourth century AD had actually begun well for the *diocese*. After his acclamation in York in July AD 306, Constantine I returned north to complete his father's campaign against the Picts. He then launched a programme to repair Britain's trunk road network, and though he next took units of the three British legions and also auxiliaries back to Trier late in the year to help defeat ravaging bands of Franks, these soon returned. Southern (2013, 306) suggests he again visited Britain in AD 307 for an unknown reason, while Eusebius of Caesarea also says in a panegyric that Constantine campaigned in Britain against an unknown enemy between AD 312 and AD 314 (*De Vita Constantini*, 1.8, 25).

Enter the Areani

The primary sources are then silent about events in Britain until the reign of Constantine I's son Constans (AD 337 to AD 350). He'd become joint-emperor along with his brothers Constantine II and Constantius II after their father's death in AD 337, and was initially given responsibility for Italy and North Africa. However, Constans' troops murdered the former in AD 340 and from that point until his own death in AD 350 Constans ruled the whole western Empire.

His first major campaign of the AD 340s was against the Germanic Franks in AD 342 where he successfully expelled an incursion into Gaul. He is then detailed making his famous maritime winter crossing to Britain to deal with some kind of emergency in January or February AD 343. We have little detail of what the issue in the *diocese* was to attract the direct attention of the emperor himself, but contemporary writers did note how dangerous a voyage this was at that time of year. One retrospective passage in Ammianus Marcellinus briefly alludes to the visit having to do with the *areani*, the first reference we have to these frontier scouts who he says were based in the far north where they performed the same role fulfilled by contemporary *exploratores*, providing strategic intelligence for the military headquarters based in York. We have little further detail of who these mysterious warriors were except they seem to have operated deep in 'barbaricum' as the Romans would have styled the territory north of Hadrian's Wall, carrying out operations specifically in the Scottish Borders, Fife and Upper Midland Valley. They may also have operated in Ireland given by this time it was a base for the increasing threat of Irish piracy in the *diocese* of Britannia. The origins of the name *areani* is unknown, although some have speculated it is a derivative of the Brythonic name for 'the secret ones'.

Based on the detail we have in the few references to the *areani*, it seems likely they were an irregular force akin to the *foederates* who operated alongside regular troops in *comitatenses* field armies and with the *limitanii* on the *limes*. How their role differed from the *exploratores*, who we know were still based in the far north of Britain at this time, is unclear. It may simply be the fact that they were irregulars. If so, they were clearly recruited north of Hadrian's Wall, though the identity of the peoples living there by this time is unclear. Early in the Principate, the various tribes in the lowlands of modern Scotland included the Votadini in the eastern Scottish Borders, the Selgovae in the central Borders, the Novantae in the western Borders, the Dumnonii around the Clyde, and the Epidii in the Mull of Kintyre. By the end of the second century AD many of these tribes, and those further north, had coalesced into two huge confederations, these the Maeatae either side of the Clyde-Forth line, and above them the Caledonians. Both proved ferocious opponents to Septimius Severus in his two attempts to conquer Scotland in AD 209 and AD 210, and it was only through the deployment of a campaigning force of 57,000 men that Severus and his sons Caracalla and Geta could eventually claim some kind of victory (Elliott, 2018a, 145). Late in the Roman occupation of Britain, the Picts then came to dominate the far north of Scotland down to the Midland Valley, including Fife, though we have no detail of who was living in the Scottish Borders by this time. The Picts are detailed in full in Appendix 1.

We do know the *areani* excelled at night-time operations, and here the late sixth or early seventh century AD *Strategikon* military manual provides near contemporary insight into how the Romans of late antiquity engaged in such operations. This book is a practical manual for commanders in the field that covers all aspects of military activity, written to codify the military reforms of the Byzantine emperor Maurice. It sets out four key factors that need to be observed by military units operating at night. These include (*Strategikon*, 9.2):

- Ensuring appropriate lighting is available using either moonlight, the stars, or torches.
- Being alert to threats that may appear at short notice given the lack of visibility compared to the daytime.
- Being quiet when nearing an enemy.
- Being very accurate with regard to timings.

Back to the chronology and Constans's mid-winter visit, others have suggested alternatives to the *areani* being the reason he risked such a dangerous maritime winter crossing. For example, Mattingly (2006, 235) has suggested the crisis may instead have involved a usurper in the south of Britain. A bronze medallion issued around this time certainly hints at a militaristic reason for Constans travelling to the *diocese*, it showing the emperor in full military uniform astride a war galley threatening the sea with a spear, with military standards adorning the ship's stern. The legend on the medallion reads 'Bononia Oceanen' which references Boulogne, almost certainly Constans' port of departure for Britain. Whatever the truth, we have no further detail. This seems to indicate matters were settled satisfactorily for the emperor, and certainly the *areani* remained in place, at least for the time being.

Britain next appears in contemporary literature in the context of the usurpation of Magnentius, commander of the *Iovani* and *Herculiani* elite *comitatenses* legions in Gaul. By this time, the military in the west had grown increasingly dissatisfied with Constans and the western field armies elevated Magnentius (who may have been born in Britain, Kean and Frey, 2005, 197) to the western throne at Autun in eastern Gaul on the 18th of January 350. This was a key location given it was the site of the numerous State-run *fabricae* manufactories which produced much of the equipment for the western military. The usurpation clearly surprised Constans who was on a hunting expedition near the Pyrenees. Knowing the emperor was separated from any military forces still loyal to him, Magnentius moved quickly and his forces soon cornered Constans near modern Perpignan where the emperor was killed. Soon the *dioceses* in Britain and Spain joined Magnentius, later joined by that in Italy, giving him control over the whole western Empire excepting North Africa. However, he failed to remain in position for long as the eastern emperor Constantius II, Constantine I's surviving son, moved quickly against him. Magnentius was soon defeated at the Battle of Mursa Major on the 28th of September AD 351 in modern Croatia, he then retreating to Gaul. He was then defeated again at the Battle of Mons Seleucus in AD 353 in south-eastern Gaul after which he committed suicide.

The major impact of the revolt of Magnentius on Britain actually occurred after the event. This was because Constantius II for some reason decided the *diocese* at the far north-western tip of the empire deserved special attention to bring it back into the imperial fold. After hunting down Magnentius' collaborators in Gaul, the emperor therefore dispatched his notorious court official Paulus *Catena* (Paul the Chain) to Britain with similar orders, as fully detailed in Chapter 3. There is no indication that the *areani* were involved in any of these events around Magnentius' usurpation, they most likely continuing their normal role helping secure the northern frontier in Britain.

The next developments in the *diocese* are recorded in the reign of Julian, the nephew of Constantine I. As detailed earlier, he'd been appointed *Caesar* in the west by Constantius II in AD 355 and features in the narrative of late Roman Britain twice. In the first instance this was in the context of his campaign against the invading Alamanni and Franks in Gaul that began in AD 355 and culminated with his decisive victory at the Battle of Strasbourg in AD 357. Here, he struggled to feed his army given much of Gaul had been lost to the Germanic invaders. He therefore turned

Areani and Later Roman Special Forces 109

westwards to Britain, free of predatory Germans, to provide grain for his troops, building a new fleet in AD 356 to transport the grain. The Greek sophist and rhetorician Libanius provides a detailed commentary on why this was necessary, saying (*The Julianic Orations*, 18.82-3):

> In the past, grain was shipped from Britain and up the Rhine. But after the barbarians took control they did not let it pass. Most of the ships, dragged onto dry land long before, had rotted. A few did still sail, but these unloaded their cargo in coastal ports, so it was necessary for the grain to be transferred on wagons instead of river, which was very expensive. Julian thought that there would be problems if he was not able to restore the traditional means of grain-shipment, so he quickly built more ships than before, and put his mind to how the river could take receipt of wheat...

The fleet Julian built here was enormous, he taking ten months to construct 400 new vessels to add to the 200 still seaworthy he had inherited in Gaul, giving him a total of 600 ships. Zosimus, who says the total was actually 800, adds they were built along the Rhine with timber felled in local forests (*New History*, 3.5.2).

However, Julian's reliance on Britain to keep his army on its successful march in Gaul may have come at a price. Even though not detailed by the primary sources, it is likely he also withdrew some troops from there to support him in Gaul given the desperate state he'd found it in. This left the western and northern defences undermanned, and unsurprisingly the Scots in Ireland and the Picts in the far north pounced on the opportunity, this event perhaps the context for the disappearance of *legio* VI *Victrix* in York which is last referenced at this time. Ammianus Marcellinus provides useful detail here, saying that in AD 360 (*The Later Roman Empire*, 20.1.1):

> The savage tribes of Scots and Picts had broken the terms of the treaty and were conducting raids into Britain, laying waste those areas close to the frontiers. Fear permeated the provinces (of the *diocese*), exhausted already by all of the disasters of previous years. Julian was over-wintering in Paris and already had enough warriors of his own: he was loath to cross the sea to help (as had Constans

earlier) as that would leave Gaul without a ruler, and the Alamanni were again threatening war.

A key point to note here is that some translators view the reference to the Scots as actually meaning the Attacotti, a fierce warrior tribe who frequently fought with the Scots and Picts. Of Scots descent themselves, they are frequently mentioned by Ammianus Marcellinus and others, more so later in the century. The Attacotti were particularly noted for their ferocious charge when trying to break an enemy battle line. The Romans were so impressed with them that they recruited them en masse into bespoke auxilia units, with four detailed in the *Notitia Dignitatum*. These were most likely *auxilia palatina* units.

Back to the narrative, instead of risking himself Julian decided to send Flavius Lupicinus, his *magister equitum* master of horse in Gaul, to Britain to shore up the western and northern defences and to deal with the incursions there. He arrived in the depths of winter after another dangerous out-of-season maritime crossing, landing at the imperial gateway at Richborough. He was accompanied by a small but highly experienced force from the Gallic field army. This included the *Heruli* and *Batavi auxilia palatina* units, and vexillations from the *Moesiaci* legion. The primary sources say these were lightly armed, perhaps indicating that they travelled without a baggage train and were more akin to a flying column designed to fire-fight the western and northern insurrections. Based on examples detailed earlier in this chapter, for example *comes* Theodosius in North Africa, it also seems likely this force included *exploratores*.

Lupicinus led his troops along Watling Street in northern Kent to the *diocene* capital of London where he used chests full of silver coinage to pay the military units already in Britain, and no doubt the loyal suppliers of grain for Julian's army in Gaul. This indicates these payments were in arrears, again indicating the scale of the crisis in the west and north of Britain. Matters settled in London, Lupicinus then set out for the west and north to tackle the problems there, no doubt commandeering the surviving field army units on the way. We have no detail about whether he was successful or not, though from a historiography perspective this isn't a surprise given Ammianus Marcellinus wasn't a fan and so would certainly be reticent about giving any praise. For example he describes

Lupicinus as (*The Later Roman Empire*, 20.1.2) 'a warlike man and skilled in military affairs, but apt to boast and talk in the style of a tragic hero. It was long a matter of debate whether his greed predominated over his cruelty or the reverse.'

However triumphant he was, Lupicinus didn't stay in Britain long enough to enjoy the fruits of his labour. This was because of the dramatic events in the east detailed earlier where, in the wake of his stalemate against the Sassanid Persians, Constantius II had called for reinforcements from Julian in the west to join him in the east. This saw the *Caesar* in Paris elevated by his troops to *augustus*, a direct challenge to Constantius II. This now put Julian in a dilemma with regard to Britain as he knew that Lupicinus, still campaigning there, was loyal to Constantius and would view him as a usurper. Ammianus Marcellinus provides more detail here, saying (*The Later Roman Empire*, 20.9.9):

> Lupicinus was an arrogant man with ideas above his station, and there were concerns that if he heard the news from across the Channel he might stage a coup. So an official was dispatched to Boulogne to keep close watch and stop anyone from crossing the channel. As a result Lupicinus returned before he could learn what had happened and was unable to cause any unrest.

It seems here that the shrewd Julian allowed Lupicinus to complete his mission in Britain, and then promptly arrested him when he arrived back in Boulogne. However, Lupicinus wasn't out of imperial favour for long, with his career back on track after Julian's untimely death fighting the Parthians in AD 363. He ultimately rose to the consulship in Rome in AD 367. Meanwhile, once more we have no references to the *areani* being engaged in military activities in Britain at this time.

Julian's legacy in Britain after Lupicinus' campaign should have been continued open ocean control of the North Sea, and of the littoral zone around the British coastline, given the huge navy he'd gathered while in Gaul. However, once more the cost of keeping a fleet-in-being proved too much, and it was soon disbanded. Britain again quickly paid the price, with raiding from Germanic pirates soon on the rise once more. Then, in AD 376 a major event occurred so dramatic in scale Marcellinus Ammianus styled it the '*barbarica conspiratio*'. We know it today as the

'Great Conspiracy'. Here, it appears the *limitanii* along Hadrian's Wall, and perhaps some units even further south, rebelled. Further, it seems they were also joined by the *areani*, with some commentators even speculating they played a leading role in planning their conspiracy. This allowed Picts from two tribes in the far north, called the Dicalydones and the Verturiones, to raid deep into the *diocese*. They also bypassed any garrison units remaining loyal to Rome by using maritime transport to land warriors south of the frontier. This may have been as far south as the Humber Estuary given the series of late Roman signal stations protecting the fertile East Riding of Yorkshire at Huntcliff, Goldsborough, Ravenscar, Scarborough and Filey which may have been in existence by then. However, what made this deep incursion so much more dangerous than earlier ones was the fact that the Picts seem to have coordinated their offensive with others who had designs of Romano-British plunder. Ammianus Marcellinus provides great detail here, saying the Picts were joined by Germanic pirates, Scots from Ireland, and Attecotti warriors from south-west Scotland (*The Later Roman Empire*, 27.8.5). Quite how these very diverse protagonists coordinated their combined offensive is problematic, this perhaps the role played by the *areani*. Whatever the case, the combined offensive was initially highly successful, overwhelming the Roman military establishment in Britain.

It is worth considering how widespread the devastation in Britain was here. Given the Picts were raiding both across the northern frontier and down the east coast, much of *Britannia Secunda* was vulnerable to attack. Similarly, with the Scots and Attecotti attacking in the north-west, this province was open to attack there too. Scots raiding also impacted *Britannia Prima* in the South West, while Germanic raiding put the entire east coast under threat, ranging from *Britannia Secunda* through *Flavia Caesariensis* and down to *Maxima Caesariensis*, with even the *diocene* capital London at risk.

Though the *limitanii* and field army did put up initial resistance, the Roman troops were soon scattered. We hear nothing of the *Dux Britanniarum* after the revolt of his *limitanii*, and it seems likely he remained with any loyal Roman troops behind the impressive late Roman defences in the legionary fortress in York. The Multangular Tower visible there today next to the Yorkshire Museum shows just how sophisticated these defences had become by the late Roman period, and clearly with some justification.

Next, the primary sources say that a commander named Nectaridus, described as the *Comes Maritime Tractus*, was killed fighting the invaders somewhere in the *diocese*. This was almost certainly the *Comes Litoris Saxonici per Britanniam*, leading his own *limitanii*. Meanwhile the *Comes Britanniarum*, a man named as Fullofaudes, was also ambushed while leading the field army, and presumably also killed given we hear nothing more of him. The whole *diocese* was now open to devastation, with the various groups of invaders free to pillage at will, and with any remaining *comitatenses* and *limitanii* staying safe behind the various fort and town defences across the *diocese*.

The emperor in the west by this time was Valentinian I who was fortunately in northern Gaul campaigning against the Alamanni. Hearing the news from Britain, he quickly marched his field army troops towards the Gallic coast. He then dispatched his *comes domesticorum* Severus, who commanded his guard troops, to Britain to investigate. Severus may also have been in charge of Valentinian's *protectores domestici*.

This was a senior figure indeed, showing how serious things had become in the *diocese*. However, for some reason he performed unsatisfactorily and was soon recalled, to be replaced by the *magister equitum* Iovinus who had more military experience. He quickly assessed the situation, realized the scale of the crisis and reported back to the emperor that urgent reinforcements were needed. However, he too was recalled, perhaps because Valentinian I had fallen ill, and the emperor now turned to his leading military leader, *comes* Theodosius (referenced earlier in the context of Firmus' rebellion in North Africa). Granted the title *Comes Rei Militaris per Britanniarum* by Valentinian I for this campaign, he crossed to Britain late in the year with a small force comprising four *comitatenses* field army units, numbering around 2,000 men in total. The scene was now set for the last major Roman campaign of conquest, or rather re-conquest, in Britain.

On arrival in Richborough Theodosius immediately headed for London, but on the way had to contend with marauding bands of insurgents in the vicinity of the *diocene* capital. This shows how desperate the situation in Britain had become. What is not clear is whether these were Germanic invaders, or *bagaudae* insurrectionists. If the latter, they were most likely former Roman troops who'd fled the colours in the face of overwhelming odds. Theodosius soon caught up with them given they were weighed down with plunder, cattle and prisoners. However, instead of butchering them on the spot the *comes* actually offered them immunity, recruiting any former soldiers back into his force. This speaks volumes regarding the anarchy he was clearly facing in Britain. He then arrived in London in triumph, welcomed as a saviour by those citizens still sheltering behind its strong walls.

Theodosius' first task was to set in place a new *diocene* government which Moorhead and Stuttard (2012, 214) describe as impressive given the nature of the task at hand. At its centre he appointed an official called Civilis as the new *vicarius*, who Ammianus Marcellinus describes as 'a man of fiery temper but uncompromising integrity...' (*The Later Roman Empire*, 28.8.7). In short, just the man for the job. The *comes* then turned to the military in Britain, appointing a *legate* on his own staff called Dulcitius as the new *Dux Britanniarum* to restore the northern frontier, with the former incumbent by this time either dead or removed from office. Here the archaeological record is instructive, providing detail of Dulcitius' campaign in the north as he set about his difficult task. In particular, a significant number of Valentinian I coins have been found at Corbridge and Piercebridge north of York, showing he made use of Dere Street as he headed to the northern frontier to challenge the Picts. Similarly, coins of the same issue have been found at South Shields, showing the military supply base being used there was once more to support the offensive. It is here we find the *numerus barcariorum Tigrisiensum* detachment of Tigris boatmen operating on the River Tyne later detailed in the *Notitia Dignitatum*, perhaps an auxiliary unit supporting Dulcitius' reconquest operations. Meanwhile, we can also track Dulcitius' offensive against the Scots and Attecotti in the north-west and northern Wales, once more through coin finds of Valentinian I. These have been found at Caernarvon (Roman *Segontium*), at Maryport (Roman *Alauna*) on the Cumbrian coast, and at Carlisle.

Theodosius campaigned well into AD 368, using a series of lightning strikes to expel any remaining marauders from the *diocese*, gathering more troops as he did so. The primary sources say he led his troops in person, with Ammianus Marcellinus saying (*The Later Roman Empire*, 28.3.2):

'He scattered and put to flight various tribes, whose impatience to attack anything Roman was inflamed by the belief that they could act with impunity.'

The primary sources also say that the *comes* had to deal with an insurrection at the same time, led by a man of high birth called Valentinus who had been exiled to Britain for an unspecified crime. It is interesting in itself that the place chosen as a punishment for Valentinus was Britain, now more than ever the wild west of empire. Moorhead and Stuttard (2012, 215) say he tried to weave together an alliance of fellow exiles (again telling) and disaffected troops, aiming to launch a coup against the *comes*. However, Theodosius got wind of it, had Valentinus and the ringleaders arrested, and then sent them to Dulcitius for execution. The Latin chroniclers go further here, saying that Valentinus was actually at the heart of the 'Great Conspiracy', but we have no further evidence for this.

Order restored, Theodosius now set about rebuilding the *diocese*, putting right any damage to the built environment and restoring the frontier fortifications. Regarding the latter the entire *diocese* was given over to the labour, this indicated by a series of remarkable contemporary inscriptions on Hadrians's Wall. These show gangs of labourers rather than the military were being used, and from far afield too. Those mentioned include representatives from the Durotriges *civitas* in the south-west, the Catuvellauni in the south and the Brigantes in the north. Some of the most significant reconstruction work was carried out in the forts along the wall, including at Birdoswald (where a new civilian settlement appears in its interior, indicating the troops there had remained loyal), Housesteads, Halton Chesters and Rudchester. Meanwhile, rebuilding also occurred at Vindolanda on the Stanegate Road just to the south of the wall. Fortification rebuilding was also carried out around the coastline of the *diocese*, for example at Caernarvon and Caer Gybi in north-west Wales and at the naval base at Bitterne on the Solent. Massive new fortifications were also built around some of the key small towns in Britain that provided a local administrative function, for example gathering the *annona militaris*. Examples include Alcester (also Roman *Alauna*) in Warwickshire and *Cuneteo* on the River Kennett in Wiltshire. Moorhead and Stuttard (2012, 226) describe this overall process as a bid to build a ring of defences around the rich agricultural farmland in the south, so important in still supplying the armies on the Rhine with grain, and also to protect the means by which it was administered. Theodosius also appointed a new *Comes Litoris Saxonici per Britanniam* (given most of the coastal forts were still in operation) and *Comes Britanniarum*, and did his best to bring the military establishment in Britain up to strength once more. However, this didn't include the *areani*, who are last mentioned at this time, and in disgrace after their collusion with the conspiracists. Given units of *exploratores* were still operational in the north, Theodosius determined the *areani* were surplus to requirements and still a risk, and so disbanded them. A Roman presence north of Hadrian's Wall did continue, given the finding of large quantities of Valentinian I bronze coins at Kelso in Roxburghshire. Coins of this type are most often associated with military pay rather than the more valuable gold and silver issues used to reward or bribe local tribal leaders. However, it is unclear if the troops in question were from *exploratores* or *limitanii* units.

The End of Roman Britain

Theodosius left a strong legacy in Britain, with a stable military and civilian leadership providing a degree of security not seen for generations. However, this only lasted another thirteen years before trouble once more broke out along the northern frontier. There, in AD 382 a Romano-British military leader called Magnus Maximus appears in action for the first time. Maximus was born on the Spanish estates owned by Theodosius the Elder and grew up with the younger Theodosius, now the emperor. Southern (2013, 340) says he may actually have been a relative, and he certainly accompanied the expedition to Britain in AD 367. He is another of the great figures of later Romano-British history given he appears a central character in later narratives detailing the transition from Roman to post-Roman Britain. We don't know which military leadership post Maximus held in Britain, though given the trouble in AD 382 was in the north it seems likely he was either the *Dux Britanniarum* commanding the *limitanii* there, or the *Comes Britanniarum* leading the *comitatenses* troops in the field army. Here again the Romans found themselves in danger of being overwhelmed, with reinforcements from the continent called for. Illustrating the rapidly changing nature of the late Roman army, these turned out to be a unit of Alamanni *foederates* called the *numerus Alamannorum* who arrived to fight under their own king, Fraomarius (Moorhead and Stuttard, 2012, 230). The campaign was a success, with Maximus apparently taking the title 'Britannicus Maximus' and celebrating a great victory.

However, all was not well. Maximus had ambitions of his own, enhanced when he viewed his childhood friend Theodosius I prospering as the eastern *augustus*. In the west the emperor Gratian was becoming increasingly unpopular, especially after he took to wearing Gothic costume. This went down particularly badly with the army after their losses in the shattering defeat at Adrianople. The emperor was especially unpopular in Britain, almost certainly in the context of the demise of Theodosius the Elder at Gratian's bidding. Then, when the latter lavished recently recruited Alan *foederates* with gifts, the field army in Britain revolted and declared Maximus the new western *augustus*. He became one of the more successful British usurpers, eventually defeating Gratian who was later killed, and then carving out an empire in the west that included Britain, Gaul, Spain and North Africa, with his imperial capital at Trier. However, crucially he failed to occupy Italy after the intervention of Theodosius I, and in AD 384 settled for being recognized the *augustus* in the west, with the 12-year-old Valentinian II co-emperor in Italy.

Maximus was a shrewd man and knew he needed the support of the elites and military in the west to remain in power, paying them large donatives to ensure their loyalty. However, after four years in power he finally overplayed his hand and marched into Italy with a view to becoming sole ruler in the west. This was the pretext Theodosius I needed to act once and for all, he mobilizing a huge field army which he marched westwards to intercept Maximus. The two former friends met in battle at Aquileia in north-eastern Italy, with Theodosius I the victor. Maximus was captured and pleaded for his life but, stripped of his royal clothing, was condemned to death out of hand. Soon a messenger was heading north-west to Trier with orders to eliminate Maximus' line, with a Frankish general promptly killing his son. Such was the price of failure in a Roman civil war.

However, even in death, Maximus left a toxic legacy in Britain. When he initially departed the *diocese* in his bid for glory in AD 383 he'd taken most of the field army troops with him, and even perhaps units of *limitanii*. Though he himself may have returned to Britain in his four years in power, given gold coins were again struck in the London mint earlier founded by the usurper Carausius in the late third century AD (the last time this was officially used), it seems most of these troops didn't. Indeed, later tradition has him granting them lands on the Armorica peninsula, whether they had family back home or not. Meanwhile, the *Notitia Dignitatum* details troops from Caernarvon now stationed in the western Balkans.

With the Roman military establishment in Britain at its bare minimum (but still including the *exploratores* units detailed earlier in this chapter), the *diocese* was again vulnerable and soon the Picts, Scots and Attecotti were on the march south and east again, particularly after the death of Maximus. Further, some of the Scots arriving in Wales also started to settle, with small communities appearing on the Lleyn and Gower peninsulas in Wales from this time. Matters came to a head in AD 398, three years after Theodosius I's death, when there appears to have been one last Roman expedition to save the *diocese*. By this time the leading figure in the Roman west was Flavius Stilicho, the western *magister militum* military leader entrusted as guardian to the 14-year-old Honorius, the new *augustus* in the west after the death of his father. Whether Stilicho himself led this final expedition to Britain we do not know, but he certainly took credit for it given matters were for the last time resolved successfully in the *diocese*.

From this point we can now look to the final ending of the official Roman presence in Britain. Around AD 406 the remaining troops there declared in quick succession for usurpers called Marcus, then Gratian and finally Constantine III as the new western *augustus*. The latter proved remarkably successful at first, crossing to Gaul with the remaining *comitatenses* field army troops from the *diocese* and setting up his capital at Arles. It may have been at this time that the *numeri* of *exploratores* based at Portchester moved back to Gaul to serve under the *magister equitum per Gallium*. However, as so often with usurpers he overplayed his hand and was finally captured and executed on the orders of Honorius in AD 411. Sadly, back in Britain the Romano-British elites reacted to his withdrawal of the remaining field army troops by throwing out the Roman administrators, with the *diocese* then cut adrift from the empire, never to return. This left Britain in a dire situation, especially in the south and east, perhaps best illustrated by Hingley who argues no one was living within the walls of Roman London by AD 410 (2018, 248).

Closing Discussion

The picture painted in this chapter regarding Roman special force candidate units in the later empire is a confusing one. Here we see the *speculatores* and *exploratores* re-emerge, alongside the *protectores domestici* already considered. Interestingly, they are often referenced in the same context as *agentes in rebus* and *notarii*. To confuse matters further, we then have the first (and last) references to the enigmatic and untrustworthy *areani* in Britain.

In terms of the *speculatores*, I determined in Chapter 4 they weren't special force troops as we would define them today, though were clearly elite warriors. Here, in this later phase of the Dominate Empire, they still weren't, though their role had clearly changed. As I suggested earlier, their focus on gathering intelligence in the context of internal affairs now set them on a par with the *agentes in rebus* and *notarii*. Indeed, perhaps what we are seeing here is an instance of contemporary popular nomenclature, where the use of the word *speculator* for an intelligence operative is simply a nickname, and that in reality they actually were *agentes in rebus* and *notarii*.

Meanwhile, the role of the *exploratores* here is equally complex. Early on in their re-emergence they are clearly still the same elite strategic military-intelligence gathering resource of old. Therefore, as set out in my analysis at the end of Chapter 4, they still count as Roman special forces. However, by the end of the fourth century AD they were far more sedentary, their activities simply reflecting those of the *limitanii* who they were operating alongside. These certainly weren't special force candidates. Most likely, by then they had lost this elite status amid the final transformation of the Roman military as the empire in the west approached its end.

Finally, we have the *areani*. These have gained interest far beyond their actual profile in contemporary literature simply because of the role they played in many events popular with modern historians at the end of the Roman occupation of Britain, particularly the 'Great Conspiracy'. In reality, the limited number of mentions of them, and lack of detail, makes it difficult to assess whether they were viable special force candidates or not. However, given they were most likely irregular *exploratores* who gained their bespoke identity through notoriety, then by way of association they can perhaps be judged viable contenders for the title, at least until their dramatic disbandment.

Conclusion

Today the term special forces is so well-known that it is the first thing many people think of when they consider any kind of military operation. Indeed, if one based such knowledge on the output of modern broadcast media, it would be the only kind of military operation. However, it is a term the Romans and their contemporaries would not have recognized. Therefore, to consider whether any of the various Roman specialist and elite troop types detailed in this book were 'special', I set out in Chapter 1 four criteria to enable such a judgement to be made, detailing that to pass the test I required a balance of all four to be met. These criteria were that special forces comprised elite volunteers chosen through a demanding selection process, were uniquely trained for non-regular warfare with special skill sets and had a bespoke *esprit de corps*, were used to secure operational and strategic advantage, and when required were deniable.

First for consideration were the various regular and elite units of the mainstream military. Whether the Praetorian Guard, *scholae palatinae*, *excubitores* or *buccellarii*, I quickly determined that these didn't meet my special force criteria. Next, I examined the roles of the *frumentarii* in the Principate empire and *agentes in rebus* and *notarii* in the Dominate empire. These were the key assets used to gather state-level intelligence, but again I came to the conclusion that while they did fulfil some of my special force criteria in their various roles, they didn't meet the required balance of all four. Therefore, they were also not special force candidates.

In Chapter 4 I turned to the *speculatores* and *exploratores*, the first specialists in gathering tactical military intelligence, the second excelling at gathering strategic military intelligence. Examining the *speculatores* over the lengthy period of time they existed, it quickly became apparent that the name itself is problematic. This is because the term was used not only to describe troops carrying out the above intelligence gathering role in support of mainstream military operations, but also for 'spies' in the Principate more broadly, for military policemen and executioners, and even for imperial guards. Then later, when they re-emerge in the historical record in the mid fourth-century AD, their activities seem indistinguishable from those of the *agentes in rebus* and *notarii*. Indeed, I suggest that perhaps by that time, as the empire in the west began its decline, they were actual *agentes in rebus* and *notarii*, with the term *speculatores* simply slang for those involved in spying operations. In none of these roles, in any of these periods, do I determine that *speculatores* meet a balance of the criteria that would allow me to call them Roman special forces.

However, certainly for most of their existence, I have determined that the *exploratores* can be considered special force candidates. It is clear to me that in their activities gathering strategic-level military intelligence they were a highly capable asset used for armed reconnaissance and other clandestine work, often deep behind enemy lines. Indeed, this is the only circumstance throughout the book where we have a force with the capability to achieve relative superiority over an enemy, using their specialist skills to overcome opponents far larger in number. Only as we approach the end of the Dominate phase of empire do we then see their role begin to change, they by this time more akin to *limitanii*.

Moving on, we then have the *protectores domestici*, with our key witness Ammianus Marcellinus who served in their ranks in both east and west. Once more, here there is confusion over the actual role of troops given this title. Some were clearly elite guards who served alongside other late Roman guard units, while others were used to gather intelligence for the emperor, both at court and when on campaign. However, I determined when concluding Chapter 4 that in neither role did these troops meet the balance of criteria needed to be considered special forces.

Lastly, we have the mysterious *areani* in Britain, and by way of analogy elsewhere in the empire. As I detail, despite the lack of data regarding their activities in contemporary literature, they were most likely irregular *exploratores*. Therefore, despite their seemingly short existence, they are suitable special force candidates.

This leaves us with just one troop type from the Roman Republic and empire who we might consider special forces judged by modern standards, the *exploratores* (and by default *areani*). However, for lovers of all things special forces, do not despair. Note that here in my review of Roman specialist and elite forces I have set the bar very high when it comes to what we today call special forces. All of the specialist and elite candidates considered here were, by Roman standards, exceptional in some way, and all played a key role in the story of the Roman Republic and empire.

Appendix

Enemies of the Roman Republic and Empire

Throughout this book the various allies and enemies of the Roman Republic and empire have been referenced in the context of our search for Roman special forces. To provide further background, in this appendix I set out in detail some of the most important mentioned. For ease of access I do this geographically rather than chronologically, moving generally from west to east.

The Britons

The military system of the native Britons fought first by Caesar, and later by the empire in its various campaigns of conquest, remained the same for most of Rome's presence in the islands.

By the first century BC the main island of Britain, where Rome later carved its province, featured a dense network of tribes who were often at war with each other. Beginning in modern Kent and heading roughly clockwise, these included the Cantiaci, the Trinovantes to their north in eastern Essex, the Catuvellauni in western Essex through to Oxfordshire, the Atrebates in the Thames Valley, and the Regni and Belgae on the south coast. In the South West, one then had the Durotriges and Dumnonii, with the Dobunni and Cornovii to their north reaching into the Welsh Marches. Into Wales proper were the Silures, Demetae, Ordovices and Deceangli ranging south to north, with the Brigantes in the north of modern England, the Carvetii in the North West, the Parisi north of the Humber, Coritani south of the Humber, and Iceni in modern north Norfolk.

Heading into modern Scotland, scene of so much campaigning during the Roman occupation of the south, I have already detailed the lowland tribes in the context of the *areani* who I considered in Chapter 6. These included the Votadini in the eastern Scottish Borders, the Selgovae in the central Borders, the Novantae in the western Borders, the Dumnonii around the Clyde, and the Epidii in the Mull of Kintyre. Then above the Clyde on the west coast, going south to north, were the Creones, the Carnonacae and (at the far north western tip of Scotland) the Caereni. On the east coast around the River Tay were the Venicones, and above them in Aberdeenshire, the Vacomagi and Taexali. Broadly, throughout the Grampians, were located the Caledonii, then around the Moray Firth, again going south to north, the Decantae, Lugi, Smertae and finally the Cornacii. As detailed in Chapter 6, many of these tribes had coalesced into the two huge Maeatae and Caledonian confederations by the end of the second century AD. Then, late in the Roman occupation of Britain, the Picts came to dominate the far north of Scotland down into the Midland Valley. Additionally, the Romans also interacted with the various Scots Irish peoples of modern Ireland across the Irish Sea.

As experienced by Julius Caesar in his two incursions in 55 BC and 54 BC, Aulus Plautius in the AD 43 Claudian invasion and Gaius Suetonius Paulinus against Boudicca, native British armies featured a chariot-riding aristocracy, skirmishing cavalry riding ponies, short spear armed line of battle troops and sling or javelin armed skirmishing foot.

In terms of army size, given few native British troops were professional warriors, various sized gatherings are reported in contemporary history. For example when Cassivellaunus, likely the tribal leader of the Catuvellauni, fought Caesar he fielded 4,000 chariots at one stage, having sent the rest of his forces home. However, given he was the leader of all resistance to Caesar in the south-east of Britain, it has been estimated he could have led up to 80,000 men. Meanwhile, as set out above, Boudicca could have led a force of 230,000, including 100,000 warriors in her incendiary insurrection. However, at the other end of the scale the Caledonians who fought Agricola at Mons Graupius in AD 83 only numbered 30,000 and were easily defeated by the Roman auxilia alone.

The elite troops in native British armies were the chariot-riding nobility, these reported in many engagements through to the fifth century AD (the latter in the context of the Scots Irish and Picts). They were most popular among the tribes in the south-east and east of the main island of Britain, but were used throughout the British Isles given the status they bestowed on the chariot rider. Native British chariots featured two ponies harnessed with a yoke and breaststraps to a draft pole, a wooden fighting platform with wicker sides, and two wheels on a centrally-mounted axle.

They featured two crew members, these being an unarmed driver and the noble. The latter carried a Gallic shield that was either oval, oval with the upper and lower ends removed, or round with a central boss. All were of plank construction. The noble also wore various kinds of Gallic helmet and a chainmail hauberk. He was armed with javelins and the long iron Gallic slashing sword. Caesar, Dio and Tacitus all describe these native chariots in action, they all reporting how manoeuvrable they were and saying the Britons deliberately rode them across the front of an enemy battle line which they showered with javelins and insults. The noble then often jumped down to fight on foot, leading his own war band.

Meanwhile, British cavalry were much lighter than their Gallic counterparts described later. They acted in a supporting role to the chariots. Specifically, they skirmished with javelins, attacked flanks and pursued routers. When used in conjunction with the chariots they proved a particular nuisance for Caesar in his two incursions to Britain.

By far the biggest component of native British armies were their line of battle spearmen. Mostly farmers called up in a mass levy when needed, they were armed in a similar manner to their Gallic neighbours. The main defensive equipment was the Gallic shield, or a simpler wicker and hide design. Few wore helmets and fewer any form of armour. The main weapon was a light spear or javelin, with some troops also armed with the long Gallic slashing sword or a dagger. In Britain these warriors formed a spear wall if required, usually in a strong defensive position as with those opposing Plautius in his river-crossing battle in Kent in AD 43, and the Caledonians deploying on the steep slopes of Mons Graupius in AD 83. However, the preferred tactic was the use of natural terrain to ambush their opponents, often as part of a guerilla campaign. The Maeatae and Caledonian confederations fighting Septimius Severus in AD 209 and AD 210 provide a good example of this.

In Britain the favoured missile weapon used by skirmishers was the sling, particularly in the South West. The Durotriges and Dumnonii tribes who fought Vespasian are a good example of this. Javelin armed skirmishers are also reported, though no bowmen.

The only major change in the nature of the opponents the Romans fought in Britain came in the form of the Picts who appear from the later third century AD, they gradually taking over the territory in the north of Scotland. Picts are first mentioned in contemporary history by the writer

Eumenius in AD 297, the name referencing their propensity for body tattoos and painting themselves in woad. They were not a single tribe, but rather a confederation, as with the earlier Maeatae and Caledonians. Their armies continued to use light chariots and skirmishing light cavalry, but many of their infantry were differentially armed when compared to their predecessors. The most obvious change was a switch to a different shield design over time, these made of hide stretched across two crossed sticks held together at the juncture. Many are depicted in Pictish artwork, usually carvings on stone monuments, and are shown as small square or round designs. Axes also feature as side arms on the carvings, as do bowmen.

The Attacotti, a people who frequently fought with the Picts, are worth a final mention. Of possible Scots Irish descent, these fierce warriors are mentioned by late Roman historians such as Ammianus Marcellinus in campaigns including the 'Great Conspiracy' detailed in Chapter 6. As detailed there, they were noted for the ferocious charge.

The Gauls

The Romans fought the Gauls on numerous occasions, including those residing in Cisalpine Gaul in the north of Italy who sacked Rome in 390 BC, and their Galatian cousins in central Anatolia as the Romans conquered the eastern Mediterranean. However, it is through Julius Caesar and his Gallic conquests that we know most about their military system. Further, it is at this time we get the most insight into the use of late Republican *speculatores* and *exploratores*, and so I focus on this period here.

Caesar fought one of the most sanguineous conflicts in Roman history when he conquered Gaul between 58 and 52 BC, this including his two incursions to Britain. He himself boasted that 1 million Gauls were killed and another million enslaved as he carved out the new Roman territories there, with Caesar having to create many new legions to achieve this.

In 58 BC, looking to the north from his new province of Transalpine Gaul along the Mediterranean coast, Caesar would have seen five broad tribal groupings in Gaul and beyond. These were Gallia Aquitania in the south-west, Armorica in the west, Gallia Celtica in central Gaul, Gallia Belgica to its north, and then Germania across the River Rhine. In his campaigns to conquer Gaul he fought many of the huge tribal confederations across this vast territory, including the Helvetti in 58 BC, Belgae in 57 BC, Veneti in 56 BC and then various large-scale revolts in conquered territories, these culminating in the Great Revolt under Vercingetorix in 52 BC (see Chapter 6).

Caesar's Gallic opponents proved fearsome warriors. Broadly their military system was similar to that of the Britons across the English Channel and North Sea. This included a chariot-riding aristocracy, and line of battle infantry armed with short spears and long slashing swords. Their infantry formations were more likely than the Britons to take on the Romans in open battle. However, the major difference was with regard to Gallic cavalry who were heavily armed and armoured and charged to contact rather than skirmish. I therefore concentrate on these here.

Gallic cavalry gradually replaced their chariotry over time, though some of the latter were still in use during Caesar's campaigns in Gaul. As with the chariots, the cavalry largely comprised the Gallic nobility, they paying high prices to buy powerful horses that became prized possessions. These gave them a distinct advantage against contemporary mounted opponents. They carried substantial shields similar in design to Gallic foot troops, though had a much higher proportion equipped with iron or bronze helmet and armour, the latter usually chainmail. For weaponry short spears and javelins were carried, with most also equipped with the long Gallic slashing sword. Cavalry swords were often of much better quality than those of the infantry.

Gallic cavalry were well-trained and could perform a variety of manoeuvres on the battlefield. Their most common attack was to advance on the enemy line of battle at speed, stopping just short and unleashing a shower of javelins. If this disordered their opponents they then drew their swords and charged home. If not, the missile attack was repeated.

Gallic cavalry were well-known in the ancient world for a particularly brutal habit, namely headhunting. The first century BC historian Diodorus provides context here, saying (*Library of History*, 5.29. 4-5):

> The Gauls cut off the heads of their enemies slain in battle and fasten them about the necks of their horses. They hand over the blood-stained spoils to their attendants to carry off as booty, while striking up a paean over them and singing a hymn of victory. They nail up the heads on their houses, just as hunters do when they have

killed certain wild beasts. They embalm in cedar oil the heads of their most distinguished enemies and keep them carefully in a chest. These they display, with pride, to strangers, declaring that one of their ancestors, or his father, or the man himself, refused the offer of a large sum of money for this head. They say that some of them boast that they refused the weight of the head in gold.

Writing shortly afterwards, the Greek geographer, philosopher and historian Strabo (*The Geography*, 4.4.5) echoes these views, adding that Roman travellers in Gaul had seen many such heads, so many in fact that eventually they got used to the sight. Today, most of the evidence of this practice comes from hillfort sites, particularly in boundary ditches and next to gateways where many of the crania found display weapon injuries. It is unclear if these were placed there deliberately, or were the casually discarded heads of decapitated lower-class warriors.

One point to note here, based on contemporary sources and particularly sculpture and epigraphy, is that this practice of headhunting for trophy heads found its way into the regular Roman army once Augustus created his auxiliary cavalry units at the beginning of the Principate. The vector was clearly the Gauls used in late Republican armies as mercenaries. By way of the example, when Caesar won the final victory over his Pompeian rivals at Munda in Spain in 45 BC some of his troops erected a palisade on which they displayed the severed heads of slain opponents to intimidate any surviving Pompeains who had fled within the town walls of Munda.

By the time of the empire, auxiliary cavalry themselves are depicted in sculpture brandishing severed heads. Four prime examples include those on the Great Trajanic Frieze detailed in Chapter 4. On one panel spanning two of the slabs three auxiliaries stand with right arms raised presenting the heads of Dacians to Trajan. The style of their armour and shields indicates they are cavalry. Meanwhile another auxiliary, this time mounted, reaches down with his left hand to grasp the hair of a Dacian, his right hand holding a *spatha* ready to decapitate his opponent. Next, on Trajan's Column one of the helical friezes shows the severed heads of two Dacians impaled on poles next to two auxiliary cavalrymen as nearby legionaries build a fort. Moving on, a gruesome scene is depicted on the Bridgeness Slab, the easternmost distance slab along the Antonine Wall which records the building of '4652' paces of the then northern frontier by legionaries of the Caerleon-based *legio* II *Augusta*, the original now in the National Museum of Scotland in Edinburgh. The inscription on the slab is flanked by scenes of victory, with that on the left showing an auxiliary cavalryman riding down four natives. One has been decapitated, with his headless body slumped forward in a seated position while his head falls to the ground. Finally, on the Column of Marcus Aurelius one of the helical friezes (scene LXVI) shows the seated emperor listening to an advisor while two auxiliaries to his left distract him by holding up severed German heads.

Meanwhile, Roman military tombstones also show headhunting practices openly professed by members of auxiliary cavalry units while based in Britain. A good example is provided by the late first century AD memorial to Aurelius Lucius in Chester. This shows his groom holding up a severed head. Meanwhile, a tombstone dated to between AD 75 and AD 120 from Lancaster shows Insus, a citizen of the Treviri and trooper with the *Ala Augusta*, grasping the head of a decapitated enemy.

Isolated skulls found on Romano-British sites have also been identified as possible trophies. Skull fragments in Flavian pits at the fort at Newstead (Roman *Trimontium*) are also thought to be discarded military trophies, while the skull of a young male found in the fort ditch at Vindolanda has sword wounds to the head and has also been interpreted as a trophy. Further, at Colchester six skulls, mostly young males and with some showing trauma associated with decapitation, were found in the town ditch and have also been identified as trophies. Finally, it has recently been argued that the hundreds of severed heads found in the upper reaches of the Walbrook Valley in London dating to the AD 120s or early AD 130s are those of the victims of a mass-beheading event after some kind of insurrection in the provincial capital.

The Germans and Goths

In considering the Germans and Goths who appear so frequently in this work, I first comment on terminology. In the book the words 'German' and 'Goth' are frequently used, confusingly perhaps given that the Goths themselves were of German descent. Both words are problematic given they infer a tribal identity that in reality did not exist. While each grouping may have often shared the same blood and cultural practices, the tribes within more often fought themselves than the Romans, and indeed later in the empire provided many of the troops and military leaders in the Dominate Roman army. Even the term 'tribe' itself is problematic given many were confederations of various regional groupings. While acknowledging these issues, I retain the use of the words here for ease of reference, especially given they were terms well understood by the Romans.

The Germanic peoples of continental northern Europe were a major opponent of the later Roman Republic and Empire, and were identified by the Romans themselves as a distinct ethnic group when compared to their southerly Gallic neighbours. The Germans originated in the westward Indo-European migrations from the Pontic-Eurasian Steppe and by 3,300 BC had split off from the main migratory group to head north-west towards the southern coastline of the Baltic Sea. They are often referred to as Teutonic, Suebian or Gothic in antiquarian literature.

Writing at the end of the early first century AD, Strabo (*The Geography*, 7.1.2/ 3) provides contemporary insight into how the Romans viewed the Germans, saying:

> Now the parts beyond the Rhenus (Rhine), immediately after the country of the Gauls, slope towards the east and are occupied by the Germans, who, though they vary slightly from the Celtic stock in that they are wilder, taller, and have yellower hair, are in all other respects similar, for in build, habits, and modes of life they are such as I have said the Gauls are. And I also think that it was for this reason that the Romans assigned to them the name Germani, as though they wished to indicate thereby that they were 'genuine' Gauls, for in the language of the Romans Germani means genuine.

The last point above, referencing the Germans as 'genuine' Gauls, is most likely a literary device by Strabo reflecting what he believed was their superior martial prowess following the conquest of Gaul by Caesar in the 50s BC and the ease with which the Gallic provinces were later incorporated into the empire.

The Germanic tribes known to the Romans originated in homelands in southern Scandinavia and the far north of Germany where they had been settled for over 2,000 years following the earlier Indo-European migrations. The later Republican Romans described four broad Germanic groupings, the first being the Ingaevones. These comprised the Cimbri, Teutones and Chauci tribes. These were based in the Jutland peninsula, Frisia and northern Saxony. Another early Germanic grouping were the Irimones, these situated further to the east between the Oder and Elbe rivers. A third grouping was called the Istvaeones, later located on the Rhine and around the Weser. The final group were called the Herminones, comprising the Suebi (from whom the Marcomanni descended, see below, as well as the Quadi, Semnones and Lombards), Chatti and Herunduri tribes, these later dominating the Elbe region. All four of these early terms for the large tribal collectives gradually fell out of use as individual tribes came to be known to the Romans.

Once the German tribes began their migrations south from their original southern Scandinavian and north German homelands they carved out new territories between the Rhine and the Pripet Marshes in modern Belarus. There they slowly consolidated until they eventually coalesced into the huge confederations which caused so much trouble to the later Roman Empire, particularly after the Hunnic expansions westward from the Central Asian Steppe drove them increasingly against the Roman *limes* along the Rhine and Danube. By then six major confederations had emerged, these being the western Visigoths, eastern Ostrogoths, Vandals, Burgundians, Langobards and Franks, all later playing a key role in the fall of the Roman Empire in the west.

The early German armies faced by the Romans, for example in the Cimbrian Wars, were very similar to their Gallic counterparts though lacked chariots. The cavalry in these armies also fought in much the same way as the Gauls, though their horses tended to be smaller. However, a particular innovation of early German armies was the deployment of light troops among the ranks of their own cavalry. Armed with javelins and shields, these swarmed around the flanks of opposing troops, hamstringing their mounts if they were cavalry.

Early German infantry formations often fought in a wedge formation rather than as a standard shield wall. Most warriors wore little armour though often carried a shield, usually square in design. Their principal weapons were javelins that they carried in quantity, aiming to shower an opposing formation with volleys prior to contact. A common type was called the *framea*, which featured a narrow blade and long socket. Some German tribes also deployed troops armed with long thrusting spears in their front ranks, for example the Cherusci and the Batavians. The main side arm was the long dagger, for example the Saxon Seax, though a few warriors also carried a sword if they could afford it.

Later German armies evolved from these early troop types into formations often very different, based on regional circumstances. For example the Ostrogoths had a much higher proportion of cavalry given their close proximity to the Sarmatians and the Turkic Steppe tribes. These mounted warriors often wore armour and helmet and carried a large round shield. The main weapon was the light spear, of which a number were carried, and a long sword. Their preferred tactic was an impetuous charge to contact. Most foot troops of later Ostrogoth armies were bowmen. Meanwhile, the Vandals who eventually settled in North Africa after a long migration had an even higher percentage of cavalry in their armies who fought in the same way.

By way of contrast, Visigothic armies featured mostly foot troops still fighting in the same manner as their early German predecessors. However, a number of confederations were well-known to the Romans for their use of specific weapon types. These included the *francisca* throwing axe and *angon* armour-piercing javelin used by the Franks, the latter detailed in Chapter 5, and the *bebrae* heavy throwing spear used by the Marcomanni.

German troops of all periods were known for their blood-chilling war-cry called the *barritus*. This started in a low voice and rose to a high-pitched chilling scream. Many Roman units later adopted this in the Dominate phase of Empire when large numbers of Germans were recruited into the legions and auxiliary units, and German leaders came to dominate the Roman officer class.

The Numidians

Numidia, an ancient kingdom in modern Algeria and Tunisia, was initially divided between the Massylii federation in the east and Masaesyli federation in the west. After the Second Punic War Massinissa, the king of the Massylii, defeated Syphax of the Masaesyli and unified the whole region into one kingdom. Numidia was a hugely fertile region, with vast expanses of prime agricultural land along the coast, in the plateaus of the Atlas Mountains and in the Great Plains which separated them from the Aures Mountains on the Saharan fringe. To control the region powerful Numidian kings built a series of major fortified cities, for example

Syphax's capital Cirta perched improbably high in the Atlas Mountains. This later became the Roman provincial capital Constantine.

The Romans first came across Numidian warriors when they served as mercenaries and allies in Carthaginian armies. They were so impressed that they were soon recruited into Roman armies. Rome fought two specific wars against the Numidians, the Jugurthine War at the end of the second century BC, and then when fighting the rebel leader Tacfarinas at the beginning of the first century AD. They also participated in the Roman civil wars in the first century BC, with for example King Juba I being an ally of Pompey, while his neighbour Bogud of Mauretania was allied to Julius Caesar.

Numidian armies were famed for their skirmishing light cavalry armed with javelins. These were much sought after as mercenaries, and later once Numidia had been incorporated into the empire formed the basis of the Principate *symmachiarii* javelin-armed mounted skirmisher. The Numidians also occasionally used war elephants of the African forest type, and in the later first century BC often re-equipped their foot warriors in panoply similar to that worn by contemporary Roman legionaries.

The Huns

The Huns proved the most difficult opponent faced by the Dominate Roman military, ravaging large sections of both the eastern and western Empire in the later fourth and fifth centuries AD. Further, as they expanded from their central Asian homelands, they drove the various German and Gothic confederations to the north of the Rhine and Danube hard against, and then through, the Roman frontiers there.

A nomadic confederation of mounted tribesmen, they most likely originated from the eastern edge of the Altai Mountains and the Caspian Sea, in roughly the region of modern Kazakhstan. They are first mentioned in contemporary sources in AD 91 living in the region around the Caspian Sea, at that time simply being one of the many tribes of interest to the empire there.

However, by the later fourth century AD the Hunnic westward migration became a major problem for the Romans, with for example their territories in Thrace and Syria overrun. This threat became existential under Attila who ruled the Hunnic confederation from AD 434 to AD 453 and who raided deep into the western and eastern Empires. He was finally defeated by the western *magister militum* Flavius Aetius at the Battle of the Catalaunian Plains in AD 451. Then, after Attila's death in AD 453 his sons fought each other for supremacy, squandering their resources, with the empire Attila built finally falling apart by AD 469.

Hunnic armies, especially later when fighting the Dominate Empire, were conglomerates of Hunnic horsemen and groups of the various subject peoples they had conquered. The latter included Alans, Goths, Franks, Burgundians and Thuringians. Hunnic warriors were largely light-cavalry horsemen, with a very few (usually nobles) equipped with armour and lance as well as the bow. Unlike many contemporaries, Hunnic light cavalry often fought at close quarters, also carrying short spears and swords. The Hunnic bow was of the powerful composite type and, at around 140cm long, large for its day.

The Sarmatians
The Sarmatians were a series of peoples of Iranian origin who migrated from the Central Asian Steppe between the sixth and fourth century BC. They eventually settled in the region of modern southern European Russia and in the Balkans east of the Dacians and north of the Danube. Closely related to the Scythians, they were noted for their high standards of horsemanship. By the early fourth century BC the Sarmatians held control of most of the land between the Ural Mountains and the Don River. From there they crossed the Don, conquered the Scythians and replaced them as the dominant force in the Pontic Steppe. The Romans first encountered the Sarmatians when the latter invaded Moesia Inferior during Nero's reign in the first century AD. They then fought alongside the Dacians as allies when Trajan carried out his two campaigns of conquest there in the early second century AD, and next were allies of the various German tribes fighting Rome during the Marcomannic Wars in the later second century AD. By that time the Romans had begun to adopt Sarmatian equipment and tactics, they now also frequently recruited into the Roman military as auxiliaries. Their territory was finally overrun by the Huns when the latter passed through their lands in the AD 370s.

The principal Sarmatian tribes included the Siracae, Iazyges and Rhoxalani. The vast majority of troops in their armies were mounted lancers, these carrying a 3.5m *kontos* lance. This was held two-handed, braced across the thighs, allowing them to charge to contact at breakneck speed, even against disciplined foot. Many were also armed with a bow. Those who wore armour were clad in coats of horn scales or chainmail, as depicted on the base of Trajan's Column.

The Armenians

Armenia was originally a satrapy of the Achaemenid Persian Empire. Only superficially affected by Alexander the Great's conquests, it became a semi-autonomous region within the sphere of influence of the Seleucid Empire. Then, after the defeat of the Seleucids at the Battle of Magnesia in 188 BC, Artaxias I founded a dynasty there in his name, unifying its various territories and enlarging what became the Armenian kingdom. It then reached the zenith of its power during the reign of Tigranes the Great from 95 BC to 55 BC, briefly becoming the most powerful state in the Roman east, controlling both Mesopotamia and Syria as the Seleucid Empire began its final collapse. However, Tigranes made a fatal error in siding with Mithridates VI of Pontus in the Third Mithridatic War, earning the enmity of Rome. Defeated at the Battle of Tigranocerta by Lucius Licinius Lucullus, he later fought and lost to Gnaeus Pompey, then finally submitting to Rome. From that time Armenia, sometimes independent and sometimes not, became a buffer between Rome in the west and the Parthians and later Sassanid Persians in the east.

The Armenian army was heavily influenced by the Parthians and later Sassanid Persians. It featured fully-armoured cataphract cavalry, mounted bowmen and loose formation foot armed with short spears, javelins or bows. Tigranes also trained some foot to fight as a Hellenistic phalanx, and others as imitation Roman legionaries.

The Parthians

On a one for one basis, the Parthians were the only real near-symmetrical threat faced by the Republican and Principate Romans until the arrival of the Sassanid Persians. They were originally a Saka tribe called the Parni, its ruler Arsaces I giving the ruling dynasty its name. They invaded the region later called Parthia in northern Iran in the 3rd century BC. This brought them into conflict with the Graeco-Bactrian kingdom who they quickly defeated, they then turning their attention to the Seleucid Empire and invading Media and Mesopotamia under Mithridates I in the mid-second century BC. From there they gradually fought their way westwards, playing a major role in bringing the Seleucid Empire down and eventually coming into conflict with the Romans and Armenians. In the first instance they resoundingly defeated the *triumvir* Crassus at the Battle of Carrhae in 53 BC, and then raided the Roman east in 40 BC and 39 BC, before losing to a Roman force under Publius Ventidius Bassus at the Battle of Cyrrhestica. Over the next 250 years the Romans and Parthians then regularly raided each other's territory. For the Romans Trajan and Septimius Severus were particularly successful, both sacking the Parthian capital at Ctesiphon, with Trajan also creating his short-lived provinces of Assyria and Mesopotamia out of Parthian territory in the early first century AD. The dynasty ended when Ardashir I overthrew Artabanus IV, the last Parthian king, and established the Sassanid Persian Empire in AD 224.

The Parthian army featured an interesting combination of extremes. These included fully-armoured noble cataphract lancers and lightly-armoured skirmishing horse archers famous for their 'Parthian Shot'. The ratio in Parthian armies was usually around 10 per cent armoured shock cavalry, using the *kontos* lance, and 90 per cent horse archers using a powerful composite bow. Infantry were usually levies, often from the former Hellenistic cities in the valleys of the Tigris and Euphrates, and played little role in major engagements.

The Sassanid Persians
The Sassanid Persian Empire was founded by its first king Ardashir I when, as the ruler of Parthian satrapy of Persis, he usurped against Artabanus V, the last Parthian king. The Sassanids proved to be a true symmetrical threat against the late Principate and Dominate Roman Empire in the east, and later the Byzantine Empire.

Once in power Ardashir consolidated central control of his newly-won territory, defeating a number of early local rebellions. Then, to win the political backing of the old Parthian aristocracy, he invaded the Roman east in AD 230, penetrating deep into Roman-controlled Mesopotamia and Syria. He then demanded the Romans give back all of their former Achaemenid Persian territories, including those in Anatolia. The Romans, caught off guard, tried to negotiate but this proved fruitless and so the emperor Severus Alexander launched a campaign against Ardashir I in AD 232, finally repulsing him. However, taking advantage of the chaos in Rome at the beginning of the 'Crisis of the Third Century', Ardashir attacked again in 238. After his death, his son Shapur I continued the war through to AD 240, capturing several cities in Mesopotamia and Syria, these including Carrhae and Nisibis.

After this conflict ended Shapur I turned his attention to the east, conquering Bactria and the western part of the Kushan kingdom. War then resumed in the west when he was defeated by the Romans under the Gordian III at the Battle of Rhesaina in AD 243. The Roman emperor then campaigned down the Euphrates Valley, but was defeated by Shapur I at Battle of Meshike in AD 244. Gordian III lost his life either in or after the battle and his successor Philip I the Arab signed a peace treaty with Shapur and withdrew. However, this was not to last and in AD 253 the war resumed when Shapur I used a Roman intervention in Armenia to again attack. He conquered Armenia, killed its king and then defeated a 60,000-strong Roman army at the Battle of Barbalissos. This left Syria open to a full Sassanid invasion in which he sacked Antioch on the Orontes, the provincial capital. It was also at this time the Persians captured the fortified frontier-trading town of Dura-Europos.

Roman attempts to counter-attack between AD 258 and AD 260 then ended in spectacular failure when the emperor Valerian was captured at Edessa by Shapur I. The Persians then advanced through Cappadocia deep into Anatolia but were finally defeated by a hastily-gathered Roman force there. Shapur I was later ejected from Roman territory by their ally, king Odaenathus of Palmyra.

Next the Romans took the offensive in AD 283 under the emperor Carus, they campaigning down the Euphrates Valley and sacking the Sassanian capital Ctesiphon. Then in AD 296 the emperor Galerius was defeated at Narseh near Callinicium, but in AD 298 he again took the offensive and won successive victories. The Romans then sacked Ctesiphon again, after which they inflicted a severe peace treaty on the Persians. This caused unrest to spread throughout the Persian Empire, this finally suppressed by Sharpur II when he became emperor in AD 309. In AD 337, part-way through his long reign, he then attacked the eastern Roman Empire again which led to a series of long drawn-out conflicts in which nine major battles were fought. It was towards the end of this phase of this long-running conflict that Ammianus Marcellinus first served as a *protector* in the region.

These wars came to an end when Julian the Apostate was killed while withdrawing from a failed invasion of Persia. An unfavourable peace for Rome followed, after which the Persians turned their attention to the east where they subdued the remaining part of the Kushan kingdom. After Shapur II's death in AD 379 the Persians then consolidated their empire, with a long peace with Rome only interrupted by two conflicts in AD 421 and AD 440. In this period they also defeated repeated invasions by the Huns, though in AD 483 the Sassanid emperor Peroz I was killed when trying to drive out another Hunnic incursion. From that point, after the collapse of the Western Roman Empire, the Sassanid Persians became a principal opponent of the Byzantine Empire.

Sassanid Persian armies were largely comprised of mounted warriors. Line of battle cavalry were called Asvaran, these initially equipped in the same way as the lance-armed cataphracts of their Parthian forebears. Over time theses changed into armoured mounted horse archers, they also carrying light spears and fine quality long swords. Again as with their Parthian predecessors they also fielded large numbers of unarmoured skirmishing horse archers. To these they also added war elephants sourced in India, while most of their foot troops again comprised a levy, by this time of poor-quality spearmen.

The Jewish Revolts

The Romans fought three Jewish rebellions in the first and second centuries AD, each testing the Empire's military capability to its extreme limit. The First 'Great' Jewish Revolt broke out in AD 66. It originated with local protests against religious intolerance and then escalated into anti-taxations protests. Soon Roman citizens in Judaea were being attacked, with the empire responding by plundering the Temple in Jerusalem and executing 6,000 Jewish captives. This prompted a full rebellion, with the Roman garrison being overrun, the Roman officials in Jerusalem then fleeing. The Roman commander in Syria, Cestius Gallus, then led an army featuring *legio* XII *Fulminata* and large numbers of auxiliary units into Judaea to put the rebellion down. However, this was ambushed and defeated by Jewish rebels at the Battle of Beth Horon, with 6,000 Romans killed and the legionary *aquila* standard lost.

This event shocked the Roman world and the emperor Nero responded by putting together a large army with four legions, auxiliary units and regional allied troops. He appointed the soon-to-be future emperor Vespasian as its commander, the veteran of the Claudian conquests of Britain then appointing his son Titus (also a future emperor) as its commander. It is here we have Nero ordering his own *speculatores* imperial guardsmen to protect father and son on their line of march into Judaea (Josephus, *The Jewish War*, 3.6.2).

In AD 67 Vespasian invaded Galilee, in the first instance targeting the regional Jewish strongholds there. However, he soon returned to Rome when news of Nero's death reached him in AD 69, and it was Titus who finally besieged Jerusalem in AD 70. By this time the city was packed with thousands of rebels who'd fled the Roman predations in Galilee. These were now deployed to defend the city's three impressive wall circuits. The first two were breached within the first three weeks of the siege. However, a stubborn stand prevented the Romans from breaking through Jerusalem's third and thickest wall, it taking a further three months to finally force a breach. This resulted in a massacre of Jewish warriors and the burning of the Temple there, the latter's treasures carried to Rome where they formed the centrepiece of Titus' triumph (this recorded on his arch in the *Forum Romanum*). Following the fall of Jerusalem *legio X Fretensis* then carried out a regional mopping-up operation, finally capturing the Jewish stronghold of Masada in AD 73/74.

The Second Jewish Revolt (also called the Kitos War) broke out in the context of Trajan's invasion of Parthia from AD 114. Here, the ever-restless emperor decided to tackle Rome's 'eastern question' head-on as he sought more martial glory after his Dacian Wars. Some have argued that his motivations here were actually economic following his annexation of the key desert trading centre of Petra and creation of the province of Arabia Petraea, after which he built an extensive road network in the east called the *Via Traiana Nova* which stretched from Busra-al-Sham (Roman *Bostra*) in Syria to Aqaba (Roman *Aila*) on the Red Sea coast. This meant that the only trading route to import spices and silk from India outside of Roman control was the Parthian port city of Charax Spasinu on the Persian Gulf. Capturing this would give the Romans a monopoly in this lucrative trade.

As so often when the Romans campaigned in the east, Armenia to the south of the Caucasus Mountains was the first focus of their attention. Trajan had already shown an interest in the region when reports arrived saying that Sarmatians were arriving on the kingdom's northern borders in large numbers. The Romans feared this would turn into a flood of migrants who would destabilize their eastern provinces and resolved to use Armenia as a barrier. Trajan began planning the annexation of the kingdom, but the Parthian king Osroes I moved first, placing his nephew Exederes, the son of a favourite brother, on the Armenian throne. Trajan promptly declared war, keen to avoid the humiliation of being outmanoeuvred politically by the Parthians. This gave Osroes pause for thought, he offering to remove Exederes and replace him with another nephew called Parthamasiris. Though Trajan rejected his offer, the Parthian king followed through his suggested plan anyway, hoping it would still placate the Romans. It didn't, and it is unclear why he expected Trajan to respond positively to yet another royal Parthian nephew being placed on the Armenian throne. By now all of the Roman plans were in place and Trajan invaded Armenia in late AD 114. He quickly defeated the Armenian forces sent to confront him, together with their Parthian allies, and then killed Parthamasiris before following through on his plan to annexe Armenia as a Roman province.

Next, in AD 115 Trajan then invaded northern Mesopotamia which he quickly overran, annexing this as another new province which he called Assyria. This secured Trajan's northern flank and rear, allowing him to campaign far down the Tigris and Euphrates valleys. Here he used these vast rivers to transport much of his force, including a large siege train. The latter allowed him to quickly capture and sack Ctesiphon, before next sailing further downriver all the way to the Persian Gulf where he famously bathed in the warm waters there. To mark his success he then founded a third Roman province in the region that he called Mesopotamia, before following in the footsteps of Alexander the Great back to Babylon where he over-wintered. Writing 250 years later, Eutropius (*Breviarium*, 8.5) says that he then ordered a fleet to be built in the Red Sea with which he intended to 'lay waste' to the western coastline of India.

However, this was not to be. As ever with the Romans in the east total victory proved elusive, and later in AD 115 major revolts broke out in the region. This included the Second Jewish Revolt in Judaea, which led the Jewish populations in Aegyptus (especially in Alexandria), the twin Senatorial province of Cyrenaica et Creta to its east, Cyprus, and also Assyria and Mesopotamia, to rebel. The latter province was particularly badly hit given the large number of Jewish exiles and refugees living there following the Roman defeat of the First Jewish Revolt. Insurrections also broke out in the latter two new provinces among Parthian remnant populations where some of the wealthy former Hellenistic cities had been used to a large degree of autonomy under their former Parthian rulers. Soon Roman military resources were stretched to the limit.

The second revolt proved even more sanguineous than the first given its much wider geographic spread. It was so serious that it threatened to undo Rome's political settlement along the south-eastern shores of the Mediterranean. At first, with Trajan in Babylon, the rebels were able to massacre many Roman garrisons, officials and citizens across the region. The Romans, used to running their provinces with a light touch, always responded brutally against rebelling populations, and Trajan decided to make a specific example of the Jewish insurrectionists, slaughtering huge numbers of them. This was on such a scale that he was forced to repopulate areas now devoid of their original populations with Roman citizens to avoid good-quality agricultural land falling out of use.

The rebellion was eventually put down by the Roman general Lusius Quietus whose *nomen*, in corrupted form, later gave the war its contemporary name as the Kitos War. As the conflict came to an end he eventually chased down the Jewish leader Lukuas to Judaea where he then sentenced to death in absentia his two deputies, the brothers Julian and Pappus. These had taken refuge in the Judaean city of Lydda along with a huge number of surviving rebels and refugees. The Romans promptly put this under close siege, eventually capturing it after a vicious assault. Most of the captives were executed including the two brothers, bringing the rebellion to an end in AD 117.

However, it is the Third 'bar Kokhba' Jewish Revolt that proved the most problematic for Rome. This rebellion was named after its leader Simon bar Kokhba, a mysterious figure whose actual family name we may not know given 'bar Kokhba' seems to be an epithet meaning 'son of a star' in Aramaic. This rebellion was even more serious than either of its predecessors given that, for the first time, the various Jewish communities in the region closely coordinated their campaigning against the Romans. Led by the charismatic bar Kokhba, who many declared was a heroic messiah who would restore a united Kingdom of Israel, the Romans were soon on the back foot, with many garrisons once more being put to the sword.

In its initial stages the bar Kokhba revolt was surprisingly successful, with one contemporary report saying it resulted in the destruction of an entire Roman legion. The rebels may also have actually recaptured the city of Jerusalem, and were certainly able to secure much of the province of Judaea under their control given they eventually announced the actual creation of the Kingdom of Israel.

However, the Romans soon regrouped. Gathering resources from across the Empire, they deployed a massive army featuring six full legions, vexillations from six others, and a large number of mounted and foot auxiliary units to settle matters with the Jewish rebels across the region once and for all. Once in theatre they adopted a scorched-earth strategy that ultimately extirpated most of the rebels, laying waste to much of Judaea. In the final phase of the conflict bar Kokhba fled to his last surviving fortress which was located at *Betar*, near modern day Battir. The Romans promptly besieged him there, capturing it after a lengthy siege. All inside perished, either in the final assault or in the ensuing massacre of those captured, excepting one lone rebel who escaped. Among the dead was bar Kokhba himself.

Roman punishment for Judaea and the Jewish rebels was particularly harsh, even by their own extreme standards when stamping out a revolt. Judean society had already been shattered by seventy years of on-off civil war, with a large proportion of the population killed, dead through starvation, enslaved or exiled (note the resettlement needed after the Second Jewish Revolt detailed above). Now Hadrian permanently changed the nature of the province, renaming it Syria Palaestina and turning Jerusalem into a pagan city that he renamed *Aelia Capitolina*. In so doing he set in train a process designed to deliberately erase Jewish history, executing many surviving Jewish religious leaders and scholars, and banning the Torah and the use of the Jewish calendar. Any surviving Jews were banned from living within sight of newly-styled *Aelia Capitolina*, with Eusebius quoting Ariston of Pella in describing the impact of this (*Ecclesiastical History*, 4.6.4):

> Thus when the city came to be bereft of the nation of the Jews, and its ancient inhabitants had completely perished, it was colonized by

foreigners, and the Roman city which afterwards arose changed its name, and in honour of the reigning emperor Aelius Hadrian was called Aelia.

Given the severe dislocation caused by the three failed Jewish Revolts, only small Jewish communities remained in former Judaea, and the demography of the renamed province now shifted in favour of the non-Jewish population. From this point the remaining centres of Jewish cultural and religious life were all to be found outside of the province, particularly in Babylonia, with other minor communities scattered around the Mediterranean.

The majority of Jewish troops fighting in the revolts were irregular infantry deployed in loose formation. Most were unarmoured excepting a shield when these were available, they being armed with short spears, javelins and side arms including swords and long curved knives. However, in each revolt the rebels made use of captured Roman equipment, including artillery. Though they did stand up to the Romans in open battle, they preferred ambushes and guerrilla campaigns. Jewish troops proved particularly difficult for the Romans to defeat in sieges where they defended fanatically, on two occasions choosing suicide rather than surrender.

References and Bibliography

Ancient Sources
Apollinaris, Sidonius, *Letters Book VIII*, trans. O.M. Dalton (London: Oxford: Clarendon Press, 1915).
Apuleius, *The Golden Ass*, trans. P.G. Walsh (Oxford: Oxford World Classics, 2008).
Aurelius, Marcus, *Meditations*, trans. M. Staniforth (London: Penguin Classics, 1964).
Caesar, Julius, *The Conquest of Gaul*, trans. S.A. Handford (London: Penguin Classics, 1951).
Cato, Marcus, *De Agri Cultura*, trans. H.B. Ash and W.D. Hooper (Harvard: Loeb Classical Library, 1934).
De Rebus Bellicis Anonymi, trans. R. Schneider (Whitefish, Montana: Kessinger Publishing, 2010).
Dio, Cassius, *Roman History*, trans. E. Cary (Harvard: Loeb Classical Library, 1925).
Diodorus, Siculus, *Library of History*, trans. C.H. Oldfather (Harvard: Loeb Classical Library, 1939).
Eusebius, *Ecclesiastical History: Complete and Unabridged*, trans. C.F. Crusé (Seaside, Oregon: Merchant Books, 2011).
Eusebius, *De Vita Constantini*, trans. C.F. Crusé (Seaside, Oregon: Merchant Books, 2011)
Eutropius, Flavius, *Breviarium Historiae Romanae*, trans. H.W. Bird (Liverpool: Liverpool University Press, 1993).
Flaccus, Quintus Horatius (Horace), *The Complete 'Odes' and 'Epodes'*, trans. D. West (Oxford: Oxford Paperbacks, 2008).
Frontinus, Sextus Julius, *Strategemata*, trans. C.E. Bennett (Portsmouth, New Hampshire: Heinemann, 1969).
Gaius, *Institutiones*, trans. F. De Zulueta (Oxford: Oxford University Press, 1946).
Herodian, *History of the Roman Empire*, trans. C.R. Whittaker (Harvard: Loeb Classical Library, 1989).
Historia Augusta: Life of Pertinax, trans. D. Magie (Harvard: Loeb Classical Library, 1921).
Jerome, *The Commentaries of Origen and Jerome on St Paul's Epistle to the Ephesians*, trans. R.E. Heine (Oxford: Oxford University Press, 2002).
Josephus, Flavius, *The Jewish War*, trans. M.E. Smallwood (London: Penguin, 1981).

Justin, *Epitome of the Philippic History of Pompeius Trogus*, trans. J.C. Yardley (Atlanta: Scholars Press, 1994).
Justinian, *The Digest of Justinian*, trans. A. Watson (Philadelphia: University of Pennsylvania, 1997).
Lactantius *On the Deaths of the Persecutors*, trans. Lord Hailes (Merchantville, New Jersey: Evolution Publishing, 2021).
Libanius, *The Julianic Orations*, trans. A.F. Norman (Harvard: Loeb Classical Library, 1989).
Livy, *The History of Rome*, trans. B.O. Foster (Cambridge, MA: Harvard University Press/Loeb Classical Library, 1989).
Paulus, Orosius, *The Seven Books of History Against the Pagans*, trans. R.J. Defarrari (Washington DC: Catholic University of America Press, 1965).
Pausanias, *Guide to Greece: Central Greece*, trans. P. Levi (London: Penguin Classics, 1979).
Pliny the Elder, *Natural History*, trans. H. Rackham (Harvard: Harvard University Press, 1940).
Pliny the Younger, *Epistularum Libri Decem*, ed. R.A.B. Mynors (Oxford: Oxford Classical Texts/Clarendon Press, 1963).
Plutarch, *Lives of the Noble Grecians and Romans*, ed. A.H. Clough (Oxford. Benediction Classics, 2013).
Polybius, *The Rise of the Roman Empire*, trans. I. Scott-Kilvert (London: Penguin Classics, 1979).
Quintilian, *Institutes of Oratory*, trans. J. Selby Watson (Scotts Valley, California: Create Space Independent Publishing Platform, 2015).
Sallust, *Catiline's War, The Jugurthine War, Histories*, trans. A.J. Woodman (London: Penguin Classics, 2007).
Statius, *Silvae*, trans. B.R. Nagle (Bloomington: Indiana University Press, 2004).
Strabo, *The Geography*, trans. D.W. Roller (Cambridge: Cambridge University Press, 2014).
Strategikon, ed. and trans. G.T. Dennis (Philadelphia: University of Pennsylvania Press, 2001).
Suetonius, *The Twelve Caesars*, trans. R. Graves (London: Penguin Books, 1957).
Tacitus, Cornelius, *The Agricola and the Germania*, trans. H. Mattingly (London: Penguin Books, 1970).
Tacitus, Cornelius, *The Annals of Imperial Rome*, trans. M. Grant (London: Penguin Classics, 2003).
Tacitus, Cornelius, *The Histories*, trans. W.H. Fyfe (Oxford: Oxford Paperbacks, 2008).
Theophanes, *The Chronicle of Theophanes*, trans. H. Turtledove (Philadelphia: University of Pennsylvania Press, 1982).
Thucydides, *History of the Peloponnesian War*, trans. R. Warner (London: Penguin, 2000).

Vegetius, *Epitome of Military Science*, trans. N.P. Milner (Liverpool: Liverpool University Press, 1996).
Victor, Aurelius, *De Caesaribus*, trans. H.W. Bird (Liverpool: Liverpool University Press, 1994).
XII Panegyrici Latini, trans. R.A.B. Mynors (Oxford: Oxford Classical Texts – Oxford University Texts, 1964).
Zosimus, *New History*, ed. and trans. R.T. Ridley (Leiden: Brill, 1982).

Modern Sources
Adams, M., *The First Kingdom* (London: Head of Zeus, 2021).
Appelbaum, A., 'Another Look at the Assassination of Pertinax and the Accession of Julianus', *Classical Philology*, No. 2, pp.198–207, 2007.
Austin, N.J.E. and Rankov., N.B., *Exploratio: Military and Political Intelligence in the Roman World from the Second Punic War to the Battle of Adrianople* (Abingdon: Routledge, 1995).
Avery, A., *The Story of York* (Pickering: Blackthorn Press, 2007).
Barker, P., *The Armies and Enemies of Imperial Rome* (Cambridge: Wargames Research Group, 1981).
Bentley, P., 'A Recently Identified Valley in the City', *London Archaeologist*, Vol. 5, Number 1, pp.13–16, 1984.
Bidwell, P., *Roman Forts in Britain* (Stroud: Tempus, 2007).
Birley, A.R., *The Fasti of Roman Britain* (Oxford: Clarendon Press, 1981).
Birley, A.R., *Marcus Aurelius: A Biography* (London: Routledge, 1993).
Birley, A.R., *Septimius Severus: The African Emperor* (London: Routledge, 1999).
Birley, A.R., *The Roman Government of Britain* (Oxford: Oxford University Press, 2005).
Bishop, M.C., *The Gladius: The Roman Short Sword* (Oxford: Osprey Publishing, 2016).
Bishop, M.C., *Lucius Verus and the Roman Defence of the East* (Barnsley: Pen & Sword, 2020).
Blagg, T., 'The Roman Sculptured Stones', in Dyson, T. (ed.), *The Roman Riverside Wall and Monumental Arch in London - Special Paper No 3* (London: London and Middlesex Archaeological Society, pp.125–193, 1980).
Blagg, T., 'Building Stone in Roman Britain', in Parsons., D. (ed.), *Stone: Quarrying and Building in England, AD 43-1525* (Chichester: Phillimore, pp.33–50, 1990).
Blagg, T., *Roman Architectural Ornament in Britain* (Oxford: BAR/ Archaeological and Historical Associates Ltd, 2002).
Bland, R., 'A Hoard of Carausius and Allectus from Burton Latimer', *British Numismatic Journal*, Vol. 54, pp.41–50, 1984.
Bonner, S., *Education in Ancient Rome* (London: Routledge, 2014).
Bradley, K., *Slavery and Society at Rome* (Cambridge: Cambridge University Press, 1994).
Breeze, D.J., *Roman Scotland* (London: Batsford/Historic Scotland, 2000).

Breeze, D.J. and Dobson, B., *Hadrian's Wall* (London: Penguin Books, 2000).
Breeze, D.J. and Hodgson, N., 'Plague on Hadrian's Wall?', *Current Archaeology*, Issue 365, Vol.30, pp.28–35, 2020.
Brown, H.S., *The Command and Control of Special Operations Forces* (Monterey, California: US Naval Postgraduate School, 1996).
Browning, R., *The Emperor Julian* (Berkeley: University of California Press, 1978).
Burgess, R.W., 'Principes cum Tyrannis: Two Studies on the *Kaisergeschichte* and Its Tradition', in *The Classical Quarterly*, Vol. 43, pp.491–500, 1993.
Burnett, A., 'The Coinage of Allectus: Chronology and Interpretation', *British Numismatic Journal*, Vol. 54, pp.21–40, 1984.
Burnett, A. and Casey, J., 'A Carausian Hoard from Croydon, Surrey, and a Note on Carausius' Continental Possessions', *British Numismatic Journal*, Vol. 54, pp.10–20, 1984.
Casey, P.J., 'Carausius and Allectus – Rulers in Gaul?' *Britannia*, Vol. 8, pp.281–301, 1970.
Casey, P.J., *Carausius and Allectus: The British Usurpers* (New Haven: Yale University Press, 1995).
Connolly, P., *Greece and Rome at War* (London: Macdonald & Co Ltd, 1988).
Cornell, T.J., 'The End of Roman Imperial Expansion', in Rich, J. and Shipley, G. (eds), *War and Society in the Roman World* (London: Routledge, pp.139–170, 1993).
Cornell, T.J. and Matthews, J., *Atlas of the Roman World* (Oxford: Phaidon, 1982).
Cowan, R., 'Aspects of the Roman Field Army: The Praetorian Guard, Legio II Parthica and legionary vexillations'. Unpublished PhD thesis: University of Glasgow, 2002.
Cowan, R., *Roman Legionary: 58 BC–AD 69* (Oxford: Osprey Publishing, 2003).
Cowan, R., *Imperial Roman Legionary: AD 161–284* (Oxford: Osprey Publishing, 2003).
Cowan, R., *Roman Battle Tactics: 109 BC–AD 313* (Oxford: Osprey Publishing, 2007).
Cowan, R., *Roman Guardsman: 62 BC–AD 324* (Oxford: Osprey Publishing, 2014).
Cowan, R., *Roman Legionary: AD 284–337* (Oxford: Osprey Publishing, 2015).
Cowan, R., 'Exploratores', *Ancient Warfare*, Vol. XV.1, pp.18–21, 2021.
Cowan, R., 'Tales of the Axe', *Ancient Warfare*, Vol. XV.2, pp.8–11, 2021.
Cunliffe, B., *Greeks, Romans and Barbarians: Spheres of Interaction* (London: Batsford Ltd, 1988).
Dahm, M., 'Lessons for the Future', *Ancient Warfare*, Vol. XV.1, pp.26–35, 2021.
D'Amato, R., *Imperial Roman Naval Forces 31 BC–AD 500* (Oxford: Osprey Publishing, 2009).

D'Amato, R., *Roman Army Units in the Western Provinces (1): 31 BC–AD 195* (Oxford: Osprey Publishing, 2016).
D'Amato, R., *Roman Heavy Cavalry (1)* (Oxford: Osprey Publishing, 2018).
D'Amato, R. and Sumner, G., *Arms and Armour of the Imperial Roman Soldier* (Barnsley: Frontline Books, 2009).
Davies, J.A., 'A Hoard of "Radiate" Coins From Allington', *Archaeologia Cantiana*, Vol. 98: pp.137–144, 1982.
de la Bédoyère, Guy, 'Carausius and the Marks RSR and I.N.P.C.D.A.', *The Numismatic Chronicle*, Vol. 158: pp.79–88, 1998.
de la Bédoyère, Guy, *Praetorian: The Rise and Fall of Rome's Imperial Bodyguard* (New Haven: Yale University Press, 2017).
Elliott, P., *Legions in Crisis* (Stroud: Fonthill Media Ltd, 2014).
Elliott, S., *Sea Eagles of Empire: The Classis Britannica and the Battles for Britain* (Stroud: The History Press, 2016).
Elliott, S., *Empire State: How the Roman Military Built an Empire* (Oxford: Oxbow Books, 2017).
Elliott, S., *Septimius Severus in Scotland: The Northern Campaigns of the First Hammer of the Scots* (Barnsley: Greenhill Books, 2018).
Elliott, S., *Roman Legionaries* (Oxford: Casemate Publishers, 2018).
Elliott, S., *Ragstone to Riches* (Oxford: BAR, 2018).
Elliott, S., *Julius Caesar: Rome's Greatest Warlord* (Oxford: Casemate Publishers, 2019).
Elliott, S., *Romans at War* (Oxford: Casemate Publishers, 2020).
Elliott, S., 'Clash of the Titans: The Battle of Lugdunum, AD 197', *Ancient Warfare*, Vol. XIII-3, pp.27–35, 2020.
Elliott, S., *Pertinax: The Son of a Slave Who Became Roman Emperor* (Barnsley: Greenhill Books, 2020).
Elliott, S., *Roman Britain's Missing Legion: What Really Happened to IX Hispana* (Barnsley: Pen & Sword, 2021).
Elliott, S., *Roman Conquests: Britain* (Barnsley: Pen & Sword, 2021).
Erdkamp, P. (ed.), *The Cambridge Companion to Ancient Rome* (Cambridge: Cambridge University Press, 2013).
Fields, Nic, *Rome's Saxon Shore: Coastal Defences of Roman Britain AD 250-500* (Oxford: Osprey Publishing, 2006).
Fields, Nic, *Britannia AD 43* (Oxford: Osprey Publishing, 2020).
Frere, S., *Britannia: A History of Roman Britain* (3rd edn) (London: Routledge, 1974).
Fuhrmann, C.J., *Policing the Roman Empire* (Oxford: Oxford University Press, 2012).
Fulford, M. and Tyers, I., 'The Date of Pevensey and the Defence of 'Imperium Britanniarum.' *Antiquity*, Vol. 69, pp.109–1014, 1995.
Galeotti, M., *Spetsnaz: Russia's Special Forces* (Oxford: Osprey Publishing, 2015).
Garrison, E.G., *History of Engineering and Technology: Artful Methods* (Boca Raton, Florida: CRC Press, 1998).

Goldsworthy, A., *Roman Warfare* (London: Cassell, 2000).
Goldsworthy, A., *The Complete Roman Army* (London: Thames & Hudson, 2003).
Goldsworthy, A., *Caesar* (London: Weidenfeld & Nicolson, 2006).
Goldsworthy, A., *The Fall of the West* (London: Weidenfeld & Nicolson, 2009).
Golvin, J.C., *Ancient Cities Brought to Life* (Ludlow: Thalamus Publishing, 2003).
Graafstaal, E., 'What Happened in the Summer of AD 122: Hadrian on the British Frontier – Archaeology, Epigraphy and Historical Agency', *Britannia* magazine, Vol. 48, pp.76–111, 2018.
Grainge, G., *The Roman Invasions of Britain* (Stroud: Tempus, 2005).
Gray, C.S., *Explorations in Strategy* (Westport: Praeger Publishers, 1998).
Grygiel, J.J., *Return of the Barbarians: Confronting Non-State Actors from Ancient Rome to the Present* (Cambridge: Cambridge University Press, 2018).
Haskew, M., *Encyclopaedia of Elite Forces in the Second World War* (Barnsley: Pen & Sword, 2007).
Heather, P., *The Fall of the Roman Empire* (New York: Macmillan, 2005).
Heather, P., *Empires and Barbarians* (New York: Macmillan, 2009).
Heather, P., *Rome Resurgent* (Oxford: Oxford University Press, 2018).
Hekster, O., *Commodus: An Emperor at the Crossroads* (Leiden: Brill, 2002).
Henig, M., 'The victory gem from Lullingstone Roman villa', *Journal of the British Archaeological Association*, 160, pp.1–7, 2007.
Hermann-Otto, Elisabeth, 'Slaves and Freedmen', in Erdkamp, P. (ed.), *The Cambridge Companion to Ancient Rome* (Cambridge: Cambridge University Press. pp.60–76, 2013).
Hingley, R., 'Roman Britain: The structure of Roman imperialism and the consequences of imperialism on the development of a peripheral province', in Miles, D. (ed.), *The Romano-British Countryside: Studies in Rural Settlement and Economy* (Oxford: BAR/Archaeological and Historical Associates, pp.17–52, 1982).
Hingley, R., *Globalizing Roman Culture: Unity, Diversity and Empire* (London: Routledge, 2005).
Hingley, R., *Londinium: A Biography* (London: Bloomsbury Academic, 2018).
Holder, P.A., *The Roman Army in Britain* (London: Batsford, 1982).
Holland, T., *Rubicon* (London: Abacus, 2003).
Holland, T., *Dominion* (London: Little, Brown, 2019).
Hornblower, S., and Spawforth, A., *The Oxford Classical Dictionary* (Oxford: Oxford University Press, 1996).
Hughes, I., *Imperial Brothers: Valentinian, Valens and the Disaster at Adrianople* (Barnsley: Pen & Sword, 2013).
James, S., *Rome and the Sword* (London: Thames & Hudson, 2011).
Johnson, A., 'Alexander's Mountaineers', *Ancient Warfare*, Vol. XV.1, pp.36–39, 2021.
Jones, B. and Mattingly, D., *An Atlas of Roman Britain* (Oxford: Oxbow Books, 1990).

Kamm, A., *The Last Frontier: The Roman Invasions of Scotland* (Glasgow: Tempus, 2011).
Kean, R.M. and Frey, O., *The Complete Chronicle of the Emperors of Rome* (Ludlow: Thalamus Publishing, 2005).
Kelly, C., *Ruling the Later Roman Empire* (Harvard: Harvard University Press, 2004).
Keppie, L., *The Legacy of Rome: Scotland's Roman Remains* (Edinburgh: Birlinn, 2015).
Kiley, K.F., *The Uniforms of the Roman World* (Wigston: Lorenz Books, 2012).
King, C.E., 'The Unmarked Coins of Carausius', *British Numismatic Journal*, Vol. 54, pp.1–9, 1984.
Kiras, J.D., *Special Operations and Strategy: From World War II to the War on Terrorism* (Abingdon: Routledge, 2006).
Kolb, A., 'The Cursus Publicus', in Adams, C., and Laurence, R. (eds.), *Travel and Geography in the Roman Empire* (London: Routledge, pp.95–106, 2001).
Kulikowski, M., *Imperial Triumph: The Roman World from Hadrian to Constantine* (London: Profile Books, 2016).
Lambert, M., *Christians and Pagans* (New Haven: Yale University Press, 2010).
Lane Fox, R., *Alexander the Great* (London: Penguin, 1973).
Langenfeld, K., 'Imperial Spies and Intercepted letters in the Late Roman Empire', Society for Classical Studies Annual Meeting, Letters in the Ancient World Panel, 44.3, 2017.
Langenfeld, K., 'Forged Letters and Court Intrigue in the Reign of Constantius II', Society for Classical Studies Annual Meeting, Late Antiquity Panel, 42.2, 2021.
Le Bohec, Y., *The Imperial Roman Army* (London: Routledge, 2000).
Leong Kok Wey, A., 'Western and Eastern Ways of Special Warfare', *Special Operations Journal*, Vol.5/2, pp.143–150, 2019.
Levick, B., *Julia Domna: Syrian Empress* (London: Routledge, 2007).
Lloyd, C.D., 'The C Mint of Carausius and Allectus', *British Numismatic Journal*, Vol. 68, pp.1–10, 1998.
Lo Cascio, E. (eds), *The Impact of the Roman Army, 200 BC–AD 476* (Leiden: Brill. pp.355–70, 2007).
Luttwak, E.N., Canby, S.L. and Thomas, D.L., *A Systematic Review of 'Commando' (Special) Operations 1939-1980* (Potomac, Maryland: C&L Associates, 1982).
MacDowall, S., *Late Roman Infantryman* (Oxford: Osprey Publishing, 1994).
MacDowall, S., *Late Roman Cavalryman* (Oxford: Osprey Publishing, 1995).
McNab, C., *The Roman Army: The Greatest War Machine of the Ancient World* (Oxford: Osprey Publishing, 2010).
Marsden, P., *Ships of the Port of London, First to Eleventh Centuries AD* (Swindon: English Heritage, 1994).
Mattingly, D., *An Imperial Possession: Britain in the Roman Empire* (London: Penguin Books, 2006).

Mattingly, D., *Imperialism, Power and Identity: Experiencing the Roman Empire* (Princeton: Princeton University Press, 2011).
Matyszak, P., *Roman Conquests: Macedonia and Greece* (Barnsley: Pen & Sword, 2009).
McCaffrey, M., 'The Batavian Revolt', *Ancient Warfare*, Vol. XV.2, pp.14–19, 2021.
McHugh, J.S., *Commodus: God and Gladiator* (Barnsley: Pen & Sword, 2015).
McLynn, F., *Marcus Aurelius: Warrior, Philosopher, Emperor* (New York: Vintage, 2010).
McRaven, W.H., *Spec Ops: Case Studies in Special Operations Warfare Theory and Practice* (New York: Presidio Press, 1995).
Mihajlov, A., 'The Paris of the Cavalry', *Ancient Warfare*, Vol. XV.1. pp.12–15, 2021.
Millett, M., *The Romanization of Britain* (Cambridge: Cambridge University Press, 1990).
Millett, M., *Roman Britain* (London: Batsford, 1995).
Moffat, B., 'A Marvellous Plant: The Place of the Heath Pea in Scottish Botanical Tradition', *Folio* magazine, Issue 1, pp.13–15, 2000.
Moorhead, S., *A History of Roman Coinage in Britain* (Witham: Greenlight Publishing, 2013).
Moorhead, S., 'The Gold Coinage of Carausius', *Revue Numismatique*, Vol. 171, pp.221–245, 2014.
Moorhead, S., 'The Frome Hoard and Britain's Emperor Carausius', *ARA News*, Issue 34, pp.10–20, 2015.
Moorhead, S. and Stuttard, D., *The Romans Who Shaped Britain* (London: Thames & Hudson, 2012).
Mouritsen, H., *The Freedman in the Roman World* (Cambridge. Cambridge University Press, 2015).
Naco del Hoyo, T., 'Roman and Pontic Intelligence Strategies: Politics and War in the Time of Mithradates VI', *War in History*, Vol.21.4, pp.401–421, 2014.
Oleson, J.P., *The Oxford Handbook of Engineering and Technology in the Classical World* (Oxford: Oxford University Press, 2008).
Omissi, A., *Emperors and Usurpers in the Later Roman Empire: Civil War, Panegyric, and the Construction of Legitimacy* (Oxford: Oxford University Press, 2020).
Ottaway, P., *Roman Yorkshire* (Pickering: Blackthorn Press, 2013).
Parfitt, K., 'Folkestone During the Roman Period', in Coulson, I. (ed.), *Folkestone to 1500: A Town Unearthed* (Canterbury: Canterbury Archaeological Trust, pp.31–54, 2013).
Parker, A., *The Archaeology of Roman York* (Stroud: Amberley Books, 2019).
Parker, P., *The Empire Stops Here* (London: Jonathan Cape, 2009).
Pausche, D., 'Unreliable Narration in the *Historia Augusta*', *Ancient Narrative*, Vol. 8, pp.115–135, 2009.
Pearson, A.F., 'Building Anderita: Late Roman Coastal Defences and the Construction of the Saxon Shore Fort at Pevensey', *Oxford Journal of Archaeology*, Vol.18 (1), pp.95–117, 1999.

Pearson, A.F., *The Roman Shore Forts* (Stroud: Tempus Publishing. Oxford: BAR/Archaeological and Historical Associates Ltd, 2002).

Pearson, A.F., 'Stone Supply to the Saxon Shore Forts at Reculver, Richborough, Dover and Lympne', *Archaeologia Cantiana*, Vol.122, pp.197–222, 2002.

Pearson, A.F., *The Construction of the Saxon Shore Forts* (Oxford: BAR/Archaeological and Historical Associates Ltd, 2003).

Pearson, A.F., *The Work of Giants: Stone and Quarrying in Roman Britain* (Stroud: Tempus Publishing, 2006).

Perring, D., 'London's Hadrianic War', *Britannia* magazine, Vol. 48, pp.37–76, 2017.

Pitassi, M., *The Roman Navy* (Barnsley: Seaforth, 2012).

Pollard, N. and Berry, J., *The Complete Roman Legions* (London: Thames & Hudson, 2012).

Potter, D., *The Roman Empire at Bay, AD 180–395* (London, Routledge, 2004).

Potter, D., *Rome in the Ancient World: From Romulus to Justinian* (London: Thames & Hudson, 2009).

Reid, R., 'Bullets, Ballistas and Burnswark: A Roman Assault on a Hillfort in Scotland', *Current Archaeology*, Vol. 27, Issue 316, pp.20–26, 2016.

Reiters, R., 'Ancient Special Operations', *Ancient Warfare*, Vol. XV.1, pp.16–17, 2021.

Rodgers, N. and Dodge, H., *The History and Conquests of Ancient Rome* (London: Hermes House, 2009).

Rogers, A., *Late Roman Towns in Britain: Rethinking Change and Decline* (Cambridge: Cambridge University Press, 2011).

Rubin, Z., *Civil-War Propaganda and Historiography* (Leuven: Peeters, 1980).

Salway, P., *Roman Britain* (Oxford: Oxford University Press, 1981).

Scarre, C., *The Penguin Historical Atlas of Ancient Rome* (London: Penguin, 1995).

Scarre, C., *Chronicle of the Roman Emperors* (London: Thames & Hudson, 1995).

Schmitz, M. and Sumner, G., *Roman Conquests: The Danube Frontier* (Barnsley: Pen & Sword, 2019).

Sheldon, R.M., *Intelligence Activities in Ancient Rome* (Abingdon: Routledge, 2005).

Sheppard, S., *Roman Soldier vs Parthian Warrior* (Oxford: Osprey Publishing, 2020).

Shiel, N., *The Episode of Carausius and Allectus, with Particular Reference to Numismatic Data*. Durham Theses, Durham University, 1975. Available at Durham E-Theses Online: http://etheses.dur.ac.uk/10146/

Shiel, N., *The Episode of Carausius and Allectus: the Literary and Numismatic Evidence* (Oxford: BAR, 1977).

Sinnigen, W.G., 'Two Branches of the Late Roman Secret Service', *The American Journal of Philology*, Vol.80.3, pp.238–254, 1959.

Sinnigen, W.G., 'The Roman Secret Service', *The Classical Journal*, Vol. 57.2, pp.66–72, 1961.

Skorzeny, O., *Skorzeny's Special Missions* (Barnsley: Greenhill Books, 1950).
Southern, P., *The Roman Empire from Severus to Constantine* (London: Routledge, 2001).
Southern, P., *The Roman Army: A Social and Institutional History* (Oxford: Oxford University Press, 2007).
Southern, P., *Roman Britain* (Stroud: Amberley Publishing, 2013).
Speidel, M.P., 'Exploratores: Mobile Elite Units of Roman Germany', in *Epigraphische Studien 13*. Bonn: Sammelband, pp.63–78, 1983.
Starr, C.G., *The Roman Imperial Navy 31 BC–AD 324* (New York: Cornell University Press, 1941).
Stathakopoulos, C., *Famine and Pestilence in the Late Roman and Early Byzantine Empire* (London: Routledge, 2007).
Strong, S., 'Death, Confusion and Darkness', *Ancient Warfare*, Vol. XV.1, pp.44–49, 2021.
Suvorov, V., *Spetznaz* (New York: W.W. Norton & Company, 1987).
Thompson, E.A., 'Ammianus Marcellinus and Britain', *Nottingham Medieval Studies*, Vol.34, pp.1–15, 1990.
Tibbs, A., *Beyond the Empire: A Guide to the Roman Remains in Scotland* (London: Robert Hale Ltd, 2019).
Toner, J., *The Day Commodus Killed a Rhino: Understanding the Roman Games* (Baltimore: Johns Hopkins University Press, 2015).
Varga, R. and Bounegru, G., 'After the Batavian Revolt', *Ancient Warfare*, Vol. XV.2., pp.40–45, 2021.
Wallace-Hadrill, A. (ed.), *Patronage in Ancient Society* (Routledge: London, 1989).
Watson, A., *Aurelian and the Third Century* (London: Routledge, 2003).
Wellesley, K., *The Long Year: A.D. 69* (Bristol: Bristol Classical Press, 1989).
Wilcox, P., *Rome's Enemies (3): Parthians and Sassanid Persians* (Oxford: Osprey Publishing, 1986).
Wilkes, J.J., 'Provinces and Frontiers', in Bowman, A.K., Garnsey, P., and Cameron, A. (eds), *The Cambridge Ancient History Vol. XII, The Crisis of Empire, AD 193–337*, pp.212–268 (Cambridge: Cambridge University Press, 2005).
Williams, H.P.G., 'Carausius and his Medallions', *The Journal of the London Numismatics Club*, Vol.8, pp.30–32, 1996.
Williams, H.P.G., *Carausius: A Consideration of the Historical, Archaeological and Numismatic Aspects of his Reign* (Oxford: BAR, 2004).
Wilmott, T. and Smither, P., 'The Plan of the Saxon Shore Fort at Richborough'. *Britannia*, Vol. 51, pp.147–174, 2020.
Windrow, M. and McBride, A., *Imperial Rome at War* (Hong Kong: Concord Publications, 1996).
Zerjadtke, M., 'No Barrier to Battle', *Ancient Warfare*, Vol. XV.2, pp.26–33, 2021.

Index

Aetius, Flavius, 23
Africa Proconsularis, 49
Africae, 101
agentes in rebus, ix, 36, 50–2, 56
Agricola, Gnaeus Julius, 20, 72, 125
Ammianus Marcellinus, ix, 41, 51, 83–6
Antonine Wall, 21, 129
Antoninus Pius, 20–1
Antony, Mark, 19, 29, 31, 63
Areani, ix, 95, 105–106
Ariovistus, 63
Atrebates, 124
Attecotti, 112
Attila the Hun, 23
Augustus, emperor, xiii, 19
Auxilia, xiv, 24–7, 36
auxilia palatina, 92, 95

Battle of the Catalaunian Plains, 23
Belgae, 124
Berbers, 101
Birdoswald, 115
Bolanus, Marcus Vetius, 71
Boudicca, 125
Brandenburg Regiment, 11
Brigantes, 71, 115, 124
Britannia, 71, 101
burgi speculatorii, 62

Caerleon, 130
Caracalla, emperor, 107
Carausius, 22, 118
Cartimandua, 70–1
Catuvellauni, 115, 124–5
Centurion, 72–3, 79
Classis Alexandrina, 42
Claudian invasion, 125
Claudius, Emperor, 32, 82
cohors I *Hispanorum,* 72

cohors II *Pannoniorum,* 72
colonia Marciana Ulpia Traiana Thamugadi, 101
comes Litoris Saxonici per Britanniam, 103
comes Rei Militaris per Britanniarum, 101
comes Theodosius, 101
Comitatenses, 103–104
Commodus, emperor, 20, 33
Constans, 84, 105, 107
Crisis of the Third Century, 78, 138
Cuicul, 101

Dacia, 72, 74, 82
damnatio memoriae, 34
Danube, River, 31, 68, 72, 74, 79
Delta Force, 16
Dere Street, 65
diocese, 101
Diocletian, emperor, 78, 82
Djemila, 101
Dominate, xiii, 23, 33, 85
Domitian, emperor, 29, 32

Entebbe, 12–14
equites, 29, 94
equites dromedarii, 29–30
equites legionis, 77
equites singulares Augusti, 32
exploratores, ix, 69–70, 72, 75–6
　Origins, 69
　Later use, 100

fabricae, 25
Firmus, 101
Foederates, 106, 116
Fort, xiv
Fortlet, xiv
Fortress, xiv
Frontinus, Sextus Julius, 145

frumentarii, ix, 45–8
frumentum, 46–7

Gallienus, emperor, 80
Geta, emperor, 107
gladius hispaniensis, 19
Governor, 26
Great Conspiracy, 101, 112, 115
Greece, 63, 79
Guerilla warfare, 126

Hadrian, emperor, 72
Hadrian's Wall, 65
High Rochester, 72
Historia Augusta, ix, 64, 66

Iazyges, 135
Iceni, 124
immunes, 25
immunes librarii, 26
Isaurians, 95

Jovian, emperor, 97
Julian the Apostate, emperor, 139
Julius Caesar, 43, 64, 125, 127, 134

Lake Victoria, 14
Lambaesis, 62
Lancaster, 130
lancea, 33
lanciarii, 30
legate, 101
legio II *Augusta*, 67
legio II *Traiana Fortis*, 42
legio VI *Victrix*, 65, 109
legio IX *Hispana*, x, 71
legio XX *Valeria Victrix*, 65
legion, 31–2, 35
limes, 29–30, 64, 66, 74, 76–7, 84–6, 96, 103, 106, 132
limitanii, 90, 92, 95, 99, 102–104, 106, 112–13, 116, 118–19, 122
Lod, 13
London, 9, 12, 15, 27, 48, 67–8, 110, 112–14, 118–19, 130
Long Range Desert Group, 9
lorica hamata, 19

Lucius Verus, emperor, 20, 57
Lupicinus, 110

Macrinus, 49
magister equitum, 85, 87, 91, 110
magister militum, 23, 54–5, 85, 118, 135
magister officiorum, 34
Marching Camps, 24, 72
Marcomannic Wars, 20, 57, 135
Marcus Aurelius, emperor, 20, 57, 130
Milvian Bridge, Battle of, 34
Mons Graupius, Battle, 125–6
Moray Firth, 125

Netherby, 72
Nero, emperor, 69
Nerva, emperor, 20
Newstead, 130
notarii, ix, 36, 50, 52–3, 56, 86, 90, 96–100, 119, 121–2
Notitia Dignitatum, x, 34, 56, 102–104, 110, 114, 118
Nubel, 101
numeri, 73–5, 103, 118

officium consularis, 26, 64, 66–7
Operation Jonathan, 14
optimates, 19, 44

Pannonia, 83
Parthia, 18, 20, 29–30
Paulinus, Suetonius, 125
Pertinax, emperor, 65–6
Picts, 105, 107, 109–10, 112, 114, 118, 125–7
pilum, 19
Plautius, Aulus, 28, 125–6
populares, 19
Portchester, 103
Praetorian *equitatae*, 69
Praetorian Guard, 31
Praetorian Prefect, 33
Primus Pilus, 79
Princeps, 19
Principate, xiii, 19
protectores divinis lateris, 80–1, 93
protectores domestici, ix, 78, 81–6, 91–4, 96, 113, 119, 122

Procopius, 96–100
Procurator, 26, 32, 37, 40, 64–5
Pyrrhus of Epirus, 27

Regional Fleets, 20, 22, 42
Rhine, River, 104, 109
Rhoxalani, 135
Richborough, 110, 113
Risingham, 72, 75, 104
Rome, 17–20

Sarmatians, 135
Sassanid Persia, xii, 21–3, 29, 78–80, 85, 90, 96–7, 111, 136–7, 139
Sayeret Matkal, 13, 72
scholae palatinae, 34–5, 81, 86, 94, 121
Scotland, 21, 106–107, 122
Scottish Borders, 106–107, 124
scutarrii, 25
scutum, 33
SEAL, viii, 16
Selgovae, 106, 124
Septimius Severus, emperor, 21, 32–3, 41, 49, 64, 78, 106–107, 113, 126, 137
Severan Dynasty, 21
Severus Alexander, emperor, 21, 137
Shapur II, 85, 90–4, 96, 101, 139
Siracae, 135
Skorzeny, Otto, xi, 11–12, 71
Solway Firth, 71–2
spatha, 129
Special Air Service (SAS), viii, 8–10, 12, 14–15

Special Boat Squadron (SBS), 10, 15
Speculatores, viii–ix, 57–8, 61–70, 74–8, 82, 95–6, 99–100, 104, 119, 121–2, 127, 140
  Origins, 61
  Later use, 96
Spetsnaz, viii, xi, 3, 16
Sulla, Lucius Cornelius, 19, 31, 45

Timgad, 101
Titus, emperor, 69, 140
Trajan's Column, 33, 136
Trajan, emperor, 29, 32, 42, 69, 72, 103, 129, 135, 137, 140–2
tribunus militum, 34
Trimontium (Newstead), 130

Valentinian I, emperor, 23, 56, 98–9, 101, 113–14, 116
Velite, 30
Vespasian, emperor, 22, 33, 69
Vexillation fort, xiv, 25, 27, 62, 67, 103–104, 110, 143
vicarious, 53, 101, 114
Vindolanda, 21, 115, 130

Watling Street, 110

Year of the Five Emperors, 21, 33, 49
Year of the Four Emperors, 20, 32, 59, 69
York, 23, 65, 105–106, 109, 112, 114

Zammac, 101